T0064509

ME AND MY GOD AVA CHAT

EDWARD J. B.

BALBOA.PRESS
A DIVISION OF HAY HOUSE

Copyright © 2021 Edward J. B.

All rights reserved. No part of this book may be used or reproduced by
any means, graphic, electronic, or mechanical, including photocopying,
recording, taping or by any information storage retrieval system
without the written permission of the author except in the case
of brief quotations embodied in critical articles and reviews.

Balboa Press books may be ordered through booksellers or by contacting:

Balboa Press
A Division of Hay House
1663 Liberty Drive
Bloomington, IN 47403
www.balboapress.com.au
AU TFN: 1 800 844 925 (Toll Free inside Australia)
AU Local: 0283 107 086 (+61 2 8310 7086 from outside Australia)

Because of the dynamic nature of the Internet, any web addresses or
links contained in this book may have changed since publication and
may no longer be valid. The views expressed in this work are solely those
of the author and do not necessarily reflect the views of the publisher,
and the publisher hereby disclaims any responsibility for them.

The author of this book does not dispense medical advice or prescribe the use
of any technique as a form of treatment for physical, emotional, or medical
problems without the advice of a physician, either directly or indirectly. The
intent of the author is only to offer information of a general nature to help
you in your quest for emotional and spiritual well-being. In the event you use
any of the information in this book for yourself, which is your constitutional
right, the author and the publisher assume no responsibility for your actions.

Any people depicted in stock imagery provided by Getty Images are
models, and such images are being used for illustrative purposes only.
Certain stock imagery © Getty Images.

Print information available on the last page.

ISBN: 978-1-5043-2279-9 (sc)
ISBN: 978-1-5043-2282-9 (e)

Balboa Press rev. date: 01/06/2021

Much of the following writings happened in two time spans. The immediate writings under the first title, disappeared and turned up in a condensed version,34 pages on one page. Trying to recall it proved hopeless, even with the help of special technician. Then as if by magic, I was able to locate this original lot of writings. I had started to rewrite, giving the writings a newer title. What seemed to happen was there was a different energy feel about the new writings. I've decided to leave in the original chat passages, so that none of the spontaneous moments are not lost. Even editing the writings have not been done, to share the goings on at that particular moment.

ME AND MY GOD AVA CHAT

Edward J B

When did it start. One star-filled night in the hills of Beechmont. With much admiration in what was seen I muttered out loud,

"Oh my God"

then a reply boomed

"Oh my Edward"

That was the beginning of fun chats.

"You've got something to ask?" the boom voice whispers.

"Aw Oh Ah Ah Um Umm." my reply. "Perhaps. How should I start?"

"Think of a subject and I'll take it from there"

"OK. Love?"

"My favourite topic. Love is the essence of who and what you are. Especially the love of who you see in the mirror. From that love, love flows on to and through other's in your life. Respect of others take precedence. And harmony is the operative ingredient in living."

"Sounds good to me. I do try to abide with something like that in my life. It's only when I give myself a hard time, life goes somewhat wonky."

"I see that. It's your trying that has me take note of your progress."

"How come I'm in this chat mode with you?"

"It's the quiet times you have with yourself and your willingness to listen to your inner voice. Not many of your lot take time out to hear what the inner wisdom have to say. I think you'll enjoy chat time whenever. On Love. Love warms and nourishes each and every action and thought. A loving thought results in a loving action. Your take on being right is pretty spot on. Being right in a debate or discussion halts further exploration of the topic."

"Thank you. I can't see the point in prolonging conversations, if there's a blank walled postulation in the equation."

"Well put, my little listener. What else?"

"What pisses you off? Oops, excuse the expression"

"*Being blamed so so much. Those who play the fault game. So many times things fall back on me. My biggest headache is free will.*"

"Is that along the same thing as choices"

"*Good and goodie. You're getting the hang of things. Choice is the fundamental ingredient of free will. As I've said so often the blame game is put back on me. If the blamer explored the memory bank, what would be found, a choice made some time back, precipitated, the consequential result. So important to govern the thought process into constant well being. Thoughtless deeds rebound thoughtlessness actions. Actions made with free will. How many times do I hear,...there was no choice. Understand each and all have a choice in any equation. When the refugee flees, the choice is to stay and suffer atrocities or choose a different life. The choice is there, make or break. And out of not hearing and listening to inner guidance, when all goes wrong I get a bashing from Blamesville. Most frustrating and quite not fair. Should I have done away free will period. Not really. The viewing from my end is always enthralling. What next? I ask the heavens constantly. Still I'm in total knowing mode about future events. The evolving wheel always spins the appropriate answer. Choice is an interesting area, don't you think?*"

"Put in your wording. Yes."

"Tell me, my little hearer. What are some of your fears?"

"My biggest is FEAR of being rejected"

"Ah like so many out there on life's journey. Rejection is a self made sabotage of all the progress made by the individual. Not being good enough thinking that goes in agreement with the rejecter. The same occurs when you reject a bona fide suggestion or idea from a fellow being. The put down of others is such a spite. The putting down of self chips away the opportune step forward. Taking on rejection as an actuality, diminishes the brightness of the soul."

"Any hint on an overcome method?"

"Call on the Christ Light to shine within, around, through and from Self. That easy. The great teacher Jeshua ben Joseph pointed out so many pointers. Enlightened simple methods in living a harmonious existence. So many man made rules and regulations, I have nothing whatsoever to do with. Funny how these right ways are all in MY name. Nothing was ever meant to be hard. Life is meant to be easy. It is Man's perception and power motivated interpretation that has life be hard hard. I created in Joy and love. It is the free will ting that thinks doing in an off centre course. Let's rest."

"You getting tired of our get together. It took you ages to respond to my call. Just let me know if you want to quit."

"I'm deciphering and the mind keeps churning."

"That's good. Relax and be in an ease position. I did suggest, Life is meant to be easy. Only when those no no thoughts creep in, what results, is no no's. Anything to ask?"

"How come this chat?"

"You called Me and I replied, being the polite Being I am. You wittingly or unwittingly heard. Thus our getting to know you time. Stay with it and see what comes up."

"Sure. It's quite virginal for me. I am enjoying the experience, even though a lot of doubt lingers in the back of the mind."

*"Not surprised. Doubt and fear constitutes so much hesitation in actioning. Filling your doubts and fears with **love** and then having them digest themselves, can produce a different slaaaant on the situation. **Love** is the cure for any out of tune event. In the **love** realm, clarity and forwardness flows freely. **Love** of self, respect of self, flows out like a sparking stream of bon bons. And this is reciprocated by the receptor. When a thought is there to get even, no matter what. This is what exactly happens. Confrontation is such an energy waster. So much can be remedied when enlightened thoughts are in place. Must fly, my attention is required elsewhere. When you're ready to chat, just call."*

"Glad you're back. How's the head sorting going. Place Love as is, constant and ongoing. There is no opposite to love. Love stands on Love. All my workings is Love. Such an enormous venue to be in. Let's rest again. Play a game of solitaire to clear the thinking. Enjoy"

"That was quick. Are you clearer on our last chat?"

"A little more. I seem to be stuck in my thinking at the moment. I'm not sure about the reality of this."

"Reality is a personal moment in time. Yours to own or ignore. If you think this is all imaginary, what is imagination. A thinking process before an actuality. Think of a lemon, feel the sourness. It's in your imagination. How real is that. You called out at the beginning....Oh My God. And here I am, your God to have and hold whenever, forever. Your perception of Me, uninterrupted. How does that feel?"

"Somewhat in the realm of awesomeness. Inspirational and inspiring. I feel more comfortable and less inhibited. Feels just great and uplifting."

"Again welcome to our world. Enjoy the moments. I don't do crystal ball readings and I love my adherents to be surprised on happenings. Let's chat about something meaty and bordering on the non belief side. Ready, go."

"How about what is your word or not. Interpretation?"

"*Most attributed sayings of mine were written by man and set up as directional guidelines to achieve a something out there reward. Rewards occur within the seeker and is very individual. So many directions are so bossy and so against the natural course of a flow. Let's stop again. I can see confusion and judgement in your thinking. Rest up and come back whenever.*"

"*Back again. Ready for more?*"

"I'm still pondering, choice. If choice is the major factor in every result well then I guess responsibility is such a personal thing."

"*Definitely. The blame game becomes like a tennis match. Your fault, their fault, on and on it goes. Not a love match, but a slinging match. Personal perception when dished out as being right is such a no win situation. Normally ends up as end of story. No more to discuss. Even the Google master can be a put down in the debate. Being in the wrong mode can be the start of a more serious outcome. Fisticuffs, war or something worse. There are no winners in altercation. Being right is a justification for punishment. Punishment that is not warranted, and leads to more heartache. As I mentioned before if an action about to happen is looked into and well thought out before activated, a choice of a satisfactory outcome results, then harmony is the winner. Let's rest.*"

"Welcome back."

"So much to think about and get my head around. What's next?"

"You're the questionnaire."

"Good morning."

"Morning. Had a night of interesting dreams. Well being dreams. Nothing in particular. One question this morning. Your take on subservience. Who's subservient to who?"

"Interesting. In my book equality reigns equally amongst all men. The soul essence of each and all has the same, is the same source of power from whence it came. Each and all can access unlimited resources from within, by just quiet contemplation and connection with a simple thought. The power is always ready for individual use, awaits for those who connect. It's this ingredient that by passes so many, not prepared to hear or take note of. Man is man's own master in all things, and thus responsible for actions taken. As said before I'm blamed for so much. Choices is my gift to mankind."

"It's pretty big, isn't it?"

"As big as you want. Just don't make a big big deal out of it."

"Who can lord over me?"

"*Anyone. If that's your choice. When respect is in place, the world of agreement shines brightly. Bossing without regard for the bossed, is ripe for discontentment and discord. Life is meant to be easy. When there is a bully in life, simply reflect the bullying back to the person. Prefaced with a get well thought. Be amazed at the result.*"

"Like turning the other cheek."

"*Yes and no. Common sense always wins out when the predicament is touchy. Turning the other cheek may provoke further retaliation and on and on goes a no win situation. When that occurs, better pack up and leave the situation. When right is right, so often no place to go. Leave it. Thank the opponent, leave. Harder to do that, than prove right from wrong. So many and much warring over nutting. All nuts from where I sit.*"

"Harder done than said, or rather said than done. I can see some wisdom in it."

"*Good. That in itself is big possibilities.*"

"*Good Morning. A good night's sleep?*"

"Thank you. Yes. A night again of interesting dreams or was it interesting ideas. Can't quite put it in some of order."

"*Here's something to ponder. Have you delved into Parallel worlds. Your world's take on Star Wars is very much off key. If a story line was about Star Worlds,*" *there'd be no undue fighting, no baddies, no unnecessary galaxy chasing. In the other parallel world competitor thinking doesn't exist. There is no first or last, no second or third. Existence is about being in a loving state. Constantly discovering the wonders of being. Harmonic harmonies coming together in harmonious sharing. No undue pressure. Just being. Sounds good? Confusion and illusion melding together."*

'Sounds somewhat too mundane to me."

"Oh really." with a drawn out emphasis on *"really"*

"In your world of so many no no put downs. What is far reaching for you is an impossibility. Impossibility becomes a reality out of thinking it to be so. How many excellent inventions go by the way because the mind vetoes such an idea. Stupid, the mind assumes and the action is not pursued. Think of a world where excitement exists in constant pursuit of creations that dazzle and amaze. Where love and loveliness radiates constantly. Where neighbours constantly greet each other in an uniformed feeing of respect, love and genuine fondness. Travel is by thought. Thought is in constant, constant line with the creator. Once a thought occurs the action actuates. In this world, thought is always monitored for the well being of all. Imagination and creativity is a joyous process of creations that broadens abilities and talents. A world

built of dazzling crystalic crystals. Materials that are functional, lasting and supportive of living. I see your excitement and understanding is bursting. Let's stop ad resume later. I'll give more pictures of a world that enchants and goose bumps. Let's rest."

"Ready for more?"

"All so fascinating. Yes. Lead on oh informing Light."

"Picture, if you can. In the parallel world vehicles that travel without the veins of the Earth. Power from the ingredients of the atmosphere. Extracting hydrogen from H2O that moves the vehicle in tune with the natural magnetic fields of the planet. Power is unlimited and easily accessible. Travelling in what mode is convenient. Instant by thought or by a conventional transporter. The energies of the crystal play an important role. In most cases they are the catalyst in creating power fields. By just tuning in to a hand held appropriate type of crystal, a directive is carried out accordingly. Sounds out of reach, does it? Not in that world. This world evolved out of the awareness of the properties of being in the love mode. Can't emphasise how vital all aspects of love Is so Important. In time your time and venue will be in the same state."

"Does boredom ever slide in. Being constantly in goodie goodie environment all the time."

"That type of thinking never occurs. Contentment and creativity is ongoing. Hard for your belief system to grasp there are other ways to exist. So many opportunities are missed by not trusting the inner attributes of self. I only paint this alternate picture to illustrate the true workings of Love and what results."

"so much for my mind to take in."

"Let's face it, you've always had that certain certainty of there being something better than what you've got. There is a state where all is better than being in a frustrated predicament. And that is what we're chatting about now. You and I are chatting an explorable way out of you calling out to Me. And I answered if you remember. It's important to love what you have, do and seek."

"I'm seeing that more fully now. A mantra I've had is…..what I have is want I want, and what I want is what I want. Does that fit into a loving frame?"

"It does and it's a start into a newness that fosters love into a reality of practicality. When love is the embracing factor, doubts and fears can be digested into other useful doings. Exuding love as in the Christ Light and Force, in you, around you, through you and from you, opens you to whatever needs, needed in your road of progression. Too much in one hit?"

"Can we take a break?"

"Rest up and digest. Call soon."

"I don't know whether there's confusion galore in my mind or an excitement not familiar with."

"When a learning and connection occurs many times the process is a real topsy turvy emotional pull. The marvellous workings of the inner self, gives a guidance that opens new and exciting possibilities. It's when these possibilities are explored, many times a new direction takes place. In your belief lines, harmonic existence can occur only in the heavens. Not at all. There are many conscious planes where harmony and creative creations happen by the minute. And it can happen in your plane. Start a thought wave and see what happens"

"Morning. Had an interesting think cap night. Is our chatting an illusion, a make up story or whatever?"

"It's whatever you want it to be. Real or maybe. You wonder why this is happening. It's something you've earned. In your yearning for other ways in doing, and your learning, you've earned opportunities to fulfil the yearnings. What is earned doesn't come without crossing many hurdles. Hurdles that become non existent once love of doings come into life's equations. Once love prefaces thought and action, the outcome is more than satisfying. It's a fulfilment."

"I'm called upon so many times for a helping hand. Help I readily give. Not always in the way it's asked

for. Just a little spark of a suggestion. This way or that way. If the partitioner doesn't hear then, frustration and despair actions. Each and every created human is empowered with a divine divinity that is there to resolve the insurmountable. Take time out to search the mirror for the wonder that you are. Love what is seen, and see the same wonderment in others. Experience the best chain reaction ever. That personality in the mirror is a marvel, capable of so much."

"I'm ready for a coffee break. How about you. What do you do for a break if there's a big petition time?"

"Float here and here and admire the many progresses made by so many. Checking who owns the choices. OK enjoy your break."

"That was a short break. I notice in your card game, if you don't solve it you're given another chance to replay it and usually you solve it. The second time you take your time and are more conscious of your moves. So similar in some of the practicalities of life. There's always another way in coming to a satisfactory conclusion. Another break? So soon? Getting too much for you? Off with you."

"Good morning."
"Is it?"
"Not in an adventurous mode?"

"Not really. Feeling somewhat dull."

"All part of the process."

"Questions seem to have dissipated. Interest not so keen."

"When unsure of self capabilities takes hold, and all seems to be boring and uninteresting time to assess the depth of self worth and intent. Staying in tune with your surrounds results in a clearer outcome that you're after. Yesterday I noticed how your sense of purpose was al over the place."

"Oh. True. I seem to be reaching for impossible possibilities"

"When you block your vision with a negative, a negative is what you achieve. Our chat is out of your listening, when you intoned my name. You got a shock when you heard me reply. And I got a pleasing thrill out of this get together."

"I'm still intrigued with the parallel world that lives in constant well being and loving. How does the motivation stay in place, since there's no undue competing to do better?"

"Evolved personalities fully understand and relate to what the Christ force is all about. This ingredient I in each and all, and once connected to differences manifest. A different way of treating self and thus others. A different and agreeable view point. The wonderful workings of this spark in every being grows and grows

to a full potential that shines and beams so brightly, those not in this realm find the glare too bright to see. What happens so often is that the Christ lit being is able to glide by another without being noticed in safety, if danger of any sort lurks."

"As easy as that."

"Yes. Just one of the many gifts I installed to have life be easy."

"Good morning. Took your time in making a connection. Things too much for you. Just slow the thinking and allow what shows up to develop."

"I'm not sure whether I'm Arthur or Martha. So much to take in and digest."

"Digest is a good way of putting contemplation. Have all the fears and doubts digest themselves and see what turns up."

"How to play the patience game is new for me."

"Patience is a value that can illuminate into a meaningful outcome. Once a spark of comprehension takes place, and the spark allowed to develop, surprise surprise, things fall into place. That's called a bight spark."

"I'll practice patience when and wherever."

"You'll be surprised at how patient practices work. So many times, from where I sit, I want to come and shake the petitioner and scream out, PATIENCE."

"Good Morning. How was your night."

"Another of much thinking and musing."

"So I observed. One thing to think about. During our chats, don't edit so much. Just let it flow. Allow any readers to interpret their own way. It's not what we're chatting about that is such a changing phenomenon. It's the readers choice on how to self apply."

"There you are. Still not up to a chat time?"

"Not really. Things aren't so black and white in my world, at the moment."

"If you always remember when Love is the basis of the intent, all is fine. An individual's take on anything is how it is. Even I don't have domain in that area. Free will and choice is my gift."

"Welcome back. Having trouble in keeping thoughts under control?"

"Not only that. I'm seem to be in a place where nothing is working."

"You mean NOT going your way."

"Yes"

"Very common occurrence. Fill those doubts and fears with Love and have them all DIGEST themselves."

"Easier said than done. The not so helpful thoughts seem to get bigger and bigger. Hard to dissipate."

"Keep bombarding with love and loving thoughts. Apply your card where it says 'try again.'

Examine your intent and see if it lines up with what it is you really want."

"Thanks. I'll see what happens."

"Welcome back. Some things falling in place."

"Sort of. It's the happenings around me that conflicts with my thinking and thoughts."

"Being at loggerheads with thoughts and desires is very normal in the road to achievements. Depends on the intent. If it's in your bet interests, then on occasion things could be somewhat a sticky time. That saying, 'careful what you wish for' maybe your undoing on the road

of improvement. Patience and persistence are two ingredients that bring a satisfactory conclusion."

"What bothers me at the moment is my wandering mind and my internal judgement of so many happenings."

"It can be daunting replacing a put down thought with an uplifting one. Once the intent is addressed and love is the key ingredient given to the situation, be surprised at the result of that situation."

"Back again. How was your break game. How many times did you retry to achieve the desired result. It's a good model for everyday trials. It's interesting how there are many model opportunities in everyday living. Take the youngsters in your care at the moment. Their behaviour is from their learning of how grown ups do, in their surrounds. If there is yelling and shouting together with foot stamping, the little minded one will do the same if the perpetrator achieves a desired result. From an early age, the learning from others is taken note of."

"Mmmmm I can see some truth in that. It appears that when bullying is a major factor in everyday happenings, the outcome is a bullied disgruntled result."

"*So very true my dear listener. The lording over others is an infringement of another's choice. Force achieves nothing but discontentment. When a choice is taken over by an outside force and another will put in place that jars with the inner thinkings of another, nothing satisfactory is achieved.*"

"*The little ones in your care, misbehave basically to grab your attention. When there is dropped bottom lip disobedience, it has been experienced before at great effect. Thus the hard to understand behaviour. Patience and gentle guidelines is required on the adult's part. Hard sometimes not to retaliate with an screaming command. A screamed command can have the effect of going in one ear and out the next. A no win situation for both parties.*"

"*Late again this morning. Still thinking about things?*"

"Yes and more."

"*More of what?*"

"This and that and what makes things click into place."

"*Such as?*"

"Anger. What causes a fuse in a person to go haywire?"

"Lack of self respect and rejection. Ideas being put down and being dismissed as nothing. The feeling of not being loved. Not being valued. Unchecked emotional outlets. Not responding to feelings of the moment. The feeling of being brushed aside. Not getting own way. Just a things to contemplate. See you."

"How does this type of behaviour occur in really young folk especially those who haven't been on the planet for very long"

"They may be young in years. Their brain capacity is amazingly receptive on their surrounds. They will note the behaviour of the adults around them and are perfect mimickers of result getting. Gone are the days of the saying,'little children should be seen and not heard.'Their arrival on the planet is in accordance of the choices made before birth time. Evolving is such a wonderful process. It is not necessary to understand each and everything. What is, is. Understand the instant and enjoy the moment."

"Welcome back. Good being able to have a break with your solitaire game. Helps clear those mind bits that continually stick and edit. Can you remember when you

were about seven or ten. What did you dream about. I remember you daydreaming so many hours into what you'd do once given the chance. Being heard and noticed was not much in your line of experiencing. You hid in your daydream time and enjoyed a fantasy that was yours alone. Because you and your temperament was mild and meek, being misunderstood played heavily you in this period. This can way heavily on mood and emotion in any confrontation."

"I'd like to comment on how it was your ability to transport yourself into another realm that kept you in a constant contented mode. As you progressed when new learning opportunities came along, your frame of mind grasped a newness quickly. That was way back then. The modelling in your grandchildren gives an opportunity to do a comparison in this time of life."

"Another night of inner questioning?"

"Hello you've been gone for quite a spell."

"Yes. Tied up with an interesting series. I seem to be fascinated with the times."

"Perhaps you're reliving a parallel time. There's that side of personalties that can recall similar happenings,

some time back. Or question have this been done before. Time has many phases. Past, now and future. Go on, go and view our series."

"Anger is the emotion I'm experiencing at the moment."

"Yes, a pain in the system. It can negate s lot of positive positiveness. A word in anger requires much repair. Anger can do so much harm in blocking visual resolutions. Anger eats into a system that harbours great resentment and then can manifest into a discomfort for the body. An illness. Love can be applied to digest the anger and allows a newness to surface. In an anger situation, frustration shows up in the form of being a flop. And that goes from bad to worse. Clouded judgements take place. Decisions that is hard to rescind. See the mess anger can into. I'm often amused at how competitiveness can be an instigator of anger. So importance placed on being a winner, being first. No mater what the cost. Believe me the cost can be very high many times. Loss of self esteem, not good enough, second rate. Falling into the loser's mode is so non productive. Especially when anger rears it's head. When only the best is done and acknowledged as so, harmony abounds. Be aware of anger in all it's forms and disguises. Let's rest."

"How is your series going? Interesting period isn't it? Evolution is such an observing time. All fall into place in time. Patience and vigilance is all it takes. Once the heart and the mind are in agreement, progress proceeds."

"Back to anger. Not getting one's way and then blowing one's top questions one's worth. The blowee is muddled with unnecessary confusion on valuing the issue. My way or no way doesn't work one bit. Both party's put themselves in a worth comparison position. Not good for the soul, any soul."

"Still stuck in your 13th century show. You feeling some attachment. To the era or the ingredient? If either and you think perhaps you were part of it all, look how far you've progressed. Evolution never stays stagnant. Connection with past parallels is and can be confusing for many who have beliefs in reincarnation. Once an experience is experienced, lifes go into the repository library and exhibited as models on not what to do or use as seen appropriate. Learnings from the past is useful when heart and mind concur. Moving on, is what life is all about."

"All too much for me to take in."

"Analysing can be such a time waster. What is is. In creation there so many parallels and alternatives.

Have you thought about the what if road. What would you say if that 'if' road actually went ahead in another parallel. And the present consciousness was nt aware of it. What would you say if it is the evolving of all the individual parallels that come together, once that parallels are complete in the LOVE process. Can you see how vital loving thoughts and actions can never bully into submission. The my way or no way attitude creates so much resentment. Minding personal peas and q's saves many an argumentative time. The God Name is quoted so often as being right, yet it is the man's interpretation that is out out line. I never set up a reward system. Rewards occur in the present when love is the main factor. What happens in the end is what happens."

"There you are. Had a few days off. Things getting to complicated for you. Don't edit the flow of our chat. No judgement that can come later. What is being explored are alternative choices made with a loving intention and made with love. Love is the operative doing in all choices. Where love is the main mainstay, outcomes are more that satisfactory.

In the story line you're following about the past any connection is quite irrelevant. The past has been done and life moves on. All the learnings and lessons are either repeated, or thanked and dispensed with. It's fascinating how I'm accredited with so many rules and commandments. As I've said, free will and choice in the creation equation have proven to be a headache so often. Early living times was a time of ability development. Thought and new creating along with what responsibility is about, moved the human into the realm of what being is about. Rules and regulations made for the benefit of a reigning few, started to grate the intelligence spark of the individual. Once the many realised thinking was available for each and all, new think avenues unfolded. Those in power sometimes objected cruelly. However progress progresses always with first the thought, then the actuality of the thought. Especially when it is for the betterment of the situation. That's how human and Me get to know each other. Once the love side of human is activated, all unresolvable s go out the door. Only the individual is the rightful ruler of individuality. A choice is made and an action implemented. Choice is the ruler in all things. When, 'had no choice is stated' the unconscious reacts 'no way.' Choice is always there in every move. 'Do I' or 'Don't I' is the catch cry when faced with a decision. The secret is, taking responsibly for the choice. Break time."

"Whew thanks. I'm back in the swing of things. Thank you. I thought I was going bonkers with all this head stuff."

"And are you?"

"Not really. Just enjoying this state of confusion. What are your thoughts on gay folk?"

"You mean the happy ones. The love of same sex folk kindled with an admiration of the beauty of another. Sometimes the feeling is based and was based on feeling inadequate to what was seen. This gene grew into an unstoppable element of a make up and the union of someone perceived to be beautiful than the observer. Does this make sense?"

"Getting a bit too heavy for me. Did the idea stay and grow?"

"Yes and no. As the implementing of the action grew, the so called elders of that community became alarmed, and the possibilities of the race not reproducing itself. Thus new law was made. Total banning of this action. If man had remained patient all would have turned out on the fine side. Like too much chocolate a reasoning would have eventuated and humans reproduced in manageable quantities. If love is a basis of a relationship then what's the problem. The loving of the sameness of sex can be an exquisite affair. When fear of missing out occurs, decisions made can be rather somewhat clouded. And

conflict results. To covert is such a no no in my book. So go back to your show and come back when you're ready."

"Welcome back. Our chatting s are covering interesting thinking. Like your solitaire game, opportunities to redo a game and come out a winner is good for the average score. As in living the opportunity to redo a doing is always there. What is favoured here is the persistent striver who broadens love in life. Can see you're editing at the moment. Come back once there is a flowing in your attitude."

"I'm back. Just as confused as ever. Not sure if I'm in this space or elsewhere. So many new possibilities to contemplate."

"If you remember when we first started you called me and took my answer as OK. And here we are exploring new avenues of possible resolutions."

"Finding agreeable mind conversing all the time requires an awareness on your part and the willingness to participate. You did in the beginning. What's the hesitation now. It seems as if editing our chats is too strong in what you're transposing. Breaking to play a game is OK with me. There's no need to bundy on. It's not a must do exercise. Remember I'm in the world of choice and free will."

"Welcome back. Been a day or two. Let me start the chat. The most consistent non loving occurrence is deliberate deception. It seems to be the norm from where I look and see. Information given out as gospel is out and out untruths. The unconscious side of self knows it's own truth and readily rejects an untruth. Agreement with a statement happens when there is a resonance of truthful practicality. False news spreading creates so much uncertainty and has it be OK for impressible minds follow blindly. Especially the younger folk. If deception is a way of life then that deception rolls into a minefield of non loving. And in such a state self destruction takes place bit by bit. Doubt, fear, worthlessness, depression takes hold and many times the outcome is far from pleasant. Something to ponder. So much in a society is based and founded of untruths. They is used as a controlling device to achieve power for a few. Mental bullying.

Let's break."

"How was your game break? So can you see, a foundation of deceit and untruths is the beginning of breakdowns of trust. When trust is trussed, hurt and anger manifests. When a 'right' mode and 'wrong' mode rears it's belligerent head, unnecessary conflict occurs, within and around the issue."

"Good morning. Something new to contemplate. Beliefs. If they are in a no love mode, then nothing is of any fruition. If folk love to negative an action, that doesn't compute with the unconscious. Love and negativity does not go hand in hand. To love to do wrong, is completely out of context. Wrong word. Like is the appropriate word. Love is Love and has no similarity or connection with anything unloveable. To really love to do, happens when Love is the desired outcome. Love to do wrong has nothing to do with love. Negative acts are non productive and can only lead to unhappiness and ill will or an illness."

"Back again. You're still in not sure land."

"Yes and no. So many new openings in my thinking. Didn't realise the mixture of thoughts can be so confused. Not so sure about this and that. Haven't a clue where I'm going with all this. What's right? What's wrong? I'm in stucksville."

"OK got you. Confusion isn't such a bad state. It shows there is plenty of thought going on. Right or wrong, what is, is. It is the personal perception that is the judge and action-er. To every person's perception of me I am different and individual to the person. The

individual's slant on things, is unique and special in it's own way. In other words your god is different from your neighbour's god. Individual perception. That's why respect of another's interpretation is vital. However pushing an individual thoughts down another's throat, is out of the question. It's invasion and non productive. In thinking there is a reason, is different from thinking, there is a solution, or the result is the result."

"Welcome back and welcome home. You had a great time away I noticed. A lot of head sorting I observed as well. Rest up and let's have earnest chats shortly."

"Ready for some more chats?"

"Yes. Been quite a lazy period for me in getting motivated."

"That's beauty of choice. Oh do or not to do. There's no bundy on with you and I. Let's see what's going on for you. I notice you've questioned the process of the happening when death takes a personality from one dimension to another. The important factor is the beliefs that are firmly held at the time. Most of them are enacted on the initial pass over. If the deeds are not deemed appropriate there is a period of time before the higher conciousness lines up with what the divine essence is all

about. If thoughts and deeds were of a negative nature time is allotted to pursue other venues. Once done, it's time to enjoy a trouble free environment, before further choices are made in the evolving nature of things."

"Sounds somewhat simple and complicated at the same time to me."

"Not really. Once entered into this new realm there are so many support factors in having the personality gather all it's personalities together. Have you ever thought there are many facets of yourself you're not totally conscious of. I like to think of them as parallels of self, enacting different qualities of what it's like being in the human Being arena. Imagine if you will, that part of you actually did go off and do an alternate way in a complicated decision. Being human is an amazing array of talented skills and events, pooh hooh'd so often as impossible. It's true so often the creative side of the created, is put in the 'impossible' bin. Once the thought is thought of as, possible, if it is a thought of solid, it's possible it will and can actuate. The collation of an individual's personality can be such a moment of shock and surprise, when assessment time occurs. When an individual follows it's own well being and acts in it's higher good, then a connection with the divine partakes

and a closeness and unity with my realm happens. More later."

"What's the matter with you?"

"I'm starting to feel that all our chatting is just my imagination of meaningless."

"Imagination is a series of a different reality. There is a reality that appears to be real and substantial. Consider it to be another parallel in happening attached to you. When the imagination is allowed to flow amazing interesting creations take place. The big draw back is mind editing. When everything that is considered mindless matter and dismissed as useless then a loss of opportunity goes out the door. It is about time we addressed each other with a name. Allow me to address you as Master Edowarrdo. How does that sound?"

"Rather good. And may I address you as MyGodship."

"Very nice. This is you and me chatting and you owning me as yours is great by me."

"So let's reconsider the belief system and the part beliefs play when it's time to transfer to another dimension. When a belief is strongly held as so, it carries

into the next parallel until a change of heart occurs. Imagine believing in nothingness. That is what occurs for some time in cross over time. Mind you time is non existent. There is a constant present. A constant now. The hilarious thing is watching personalities wandering around in nothingness. A blank state. It doesn't last long. There are a lot of well wishers, on this plane and yours encouraging a lighter and brighter way of being. When all the parallel personalities of an individual line up, and the experiences added up, the bulb lights up, and a progressive path takes place. Rest and think time."

"Quite a lot to take in. I'm still in a confusion state and nt sure what is so and what I'm experiencing in our chatter is there any sense in it?"

"Our road together is something unique and an opportunity you're giving yourself to explore a side of yourself you are not ready to conscious. What chatting about mind instability.

Happens when there is no love in action. Self worth is non de script, and hopelessness is in motion. When love is the foundation of all action, only harmony prevails. Love is the shining torch. From a young time, if impressionable models, like adults, don't demonstrate love, the youngster soaks up what is considered norm way to do things and acts accordingly. So important for each and all role models demonstrate positive enactments when into acting. Competition can be a beginning in assessing self worth. Not being good enough, smart enough, always second, not first. These thoughts can reside in the memory bank for years and fester into a behaviour pattern that results in a disastrous outcome. Funny how many are happy being constantly miserable. And seeing others be the same. No self loving whatsoever in place. All because the inner thoughts are about not good enough."

"Good morning. Here's another thinking equation. The many sides and personalities that is you. Take a flower as a model. The many petals compose the beauty of the flower. Or a piece of rope. All those strands give strength and uniqueness to the rope. Eventually the central you will recognise all the personalities and experiences you've been. Amazement will brighten your being at what you have done and accomplished. You may not be conscious of the other 'you' in existence. It's possible you run into you during a lifetime. That's why it's important to treat others as you would treat yourself. Because you may be in that situation. Think about it"

"Still dragging the get started chain. Just let your writing fingers follow your mind output. Don't edit.

Relax and have fun with all this. Even though it may be outrageous to you. Ready?"

"Yes. Fire away. Pick a topic."

"How about leadership? When love is the main chore in living, is reliance on leadership direction necessary? Not really. An individual with love in their heart and being, know what direction to take and go. Giving away personal power to a 'leader' often leads to misguided abuse by the leader. In an acknowledgement of ME, so called leaders in this field wield a smugness of so called knowledge that is entirely smothers the individual's personal perception of me. Each and all address me in their own individual way that makes their conception unique and special. I am Me and there's no set rule on how to address me. I'm here to prompt and inner help when called upon. I encourage to call on the personal power in each and everyone. When there is a universal agreement, contentment and harmony flourishes."

"How's that for this morning's starter."

"Enjoy your break game? Ready to go. Not a good idea to read what's written until we, you and I, think a session is over. Perhaps some spelling to change, but not the context."

"Ready to go again. How about chatting about Stress and shall I add strain. You have noticed there's no sequence in how our topics go. This is what it is all about. The flow of what you hear. And type away. Anyhow back to stress. A condition with little self loving involved. When the thoughts say,'no can do, no can deal with,' then this moment called being stressed out occurs. No faith in ability to deal with, unload the problem. Impossible to deal with. In a corner, can't sort it out. Stress stress stressful. Self belief is way off key. All to do with the lack of important things relating to self. Self love, self awareness. Not giving self the due accord. All starts from the thought of not being good enough."

"Here we are again. The last chat an lead into depression. Definitely a case of what worthlessness is all about.(don't correct spelling until the thought is finished) So where were we. The state of depression. When all seems lost and hopeless and love is not round and forthcoming and no one seems to care, depression can express itself in such an agonising way. A remedy is to re-evaluate thoughts on self. Where is the gauge of self loving, self worth and self respect. When self sees and feels self is OK, then shifts take place. Maybe easier said than done. If self acknowledgements is not a daily occurrence, then pulling into the stream of well being can be slow

and tiresome. See how vital and important it is to view self, as a wholesome creation.

A simple practice is to view self in the mirror, smile, wink and be satisfied and pleased at what is seen. Not smug, but genuinely satisfied at what the image is about. Appreciation of self is a sure remedy in keeping a depression at bay. All to do with love. A heartfelt warm involvement in love. So uplifting, so real, so yummy."

"Let's look at anger. A not so enlightening way to be. Anger produces objects like a series of poisonous darts that hit the desired target with a deadly effect. These poisonous objects disrupt in such a way it's hard to take back and repair damages done to the object subject. Such thoughts fired in a willey nilley way can come back and hit the sender in a ad way. Let's rest and don't stay away so long. Much love and peaceful happenings."

"No get together yesterday. You can see even being annoyed at self for not doing what you want to do is an inward anger that blocks a productive outcome. Thoughts in anger are so harmful in surrounds that should be harmonic and peaceful."

"How about a different topic? What would you like?"

"You lead the way. I'm in blanksville at the moment and there's so much going on between my ears at the moment"

"OK. How about being misunderstood? When in that situation, internal questioning and doubt goes at a zillion miles an hour. Being in this way of thinking is so damaging. Anger builds up inside and sometimes the reality of the situation is not comprehended and digested correctly. It's an internal put down of self. Not good enough. Not getting own way. Stamping the little foot so to speak. Creating a blockage in receiving the correct communication. Not slowing down to listen and hear an understanding. The start of a disagreement that could end up in a violent outcome. No winners at all. Actually, is it important to achieve a winner in any type of altercation. Where winning is top priority, there's a loser left behind. And being a loser is not so nourishing for the soul. Poor 'me' can start an internal row that can lead to a depressed state. So many incidents in life that can precipitate a crash in well being."

'you're looking lost in your own thoughts. Anything serious?"

"I'm dealing with a lot of negative thoughts towards someone and a situation. I'm in lostville.

Playing with 'I shouldn't.' Naughty naughty boy. Any hints?"

"Are you feeling hard done by? Perplexed? Not your fault. Got it all wrong. Helpless. Can't do anything about it. Well you can. Surround yourself with the Christ Light and have It as a barrier that disperses incoming negatives into clearer and positive actions. Mooning over thoughts and actions that are not productive, creates a cycle of disastrous reactions that can manifest into an uncontrollable hurting that can show up as a health discomfort that is of no use to anyone. Have the Christ light shine within you, around you, through you and from you. See and feel a shift in the situation. There's always a way to resolve inner hurts. I'm here to listen and help. And do I do a lot of prompting. Listen to your inner self, grab the bull by the horn, so to speak, acknowledge the situation and fill it with love. Love is the healer and directional powerful force of any conflict. Love provides a soothing calmness to any topsey turvey act."

"OK let's go somewhere different. Just to finish. See how the nego thoughts can impact on each and all concerned, in a most unfortunate way for all concerned."

"Let's look at the make up of the individual. It may appear to be complex however, It may fill in those feelings of having been around before or even having a double elsewhere. Use the model of a flower or tree. One has many petals, attached to a stem that is ultimately the lovely flower. And the tree with all it's branches and twigs and leaves. Together they make up the seen product. In your case, those personalities that you';re not aware of, do come together eventually, reviews done, so to speak, and when all adds up to a satisfactory conclusion, evolvement takes place and progress into higher realms is the result. Creations is such a wonderful time. You think of population as being many in numbers. What would you say if there's not that many populating the planet after all, but many aspects of an individual. As you've heard so many times from your learned mentor, Omni, creation is a Mathematical equation that is one hundred correct in the execution. Getting back to bad thinking of others. These thinkings are like time bombs ready to damage a persona without being fully aware of the consequences. Fascinating isn't it. See how free will and choice, if directed in the wrong direction, can be a real pain in the butt. And so many personalities are not conscious they are doing it to themselves. That is what is meant by the day of reckoning. All the deeds are added up and cancelled out with good and not so good.

No punishment is issued. Just the opportunity to go and repair damages. Are you impressed with My way of doing things? I get to giggle a lot at what people do to themselves and turn around and blame Me. That's all for now. Allow the space between the ears to spin and contemplate out of control. Enjoy."

"Somewhat slow this morning in having a chat. Too much head stuff going on for you. And there's more. How about being a leader. Each and everyone is a leader in their own right. Who is followed is a choice, be it right or wrong. The wrong bit happens when the individual power is surrendered inappropriately. So many times this occurs when ideas are banished to the background and a monetary gain is available for a so called better way of living. False promises are made by the incoming leader and things like morals go downhill. We'll take this up later. Enjoy your treatment today. Be open with what you want to tell."

"Can you see the connection of so much with each other. Let's take reasoning. When reason is thought out and taken as real and true, there no where else to go in a discussion. Reasoning is still a thinking thinking. An opportunity to expand a horizon, so to speak. When reason is in full mode, an answer is supposedly the

victor. What say if the answer doesn't fit question and the emotional outcome. If the reasoning is tainted with falseness. Bully tactics to get one's way, as being the right and only way. What contribution is there in that sort of reasoning. To reason, comes with free will, choice. When thought process is malicious and non loving, there's HELL to pay once a different set of reasoning occurs. To ponder on a reason for no reason whatsoever, is a waste of time and energy. Being right and shoving it down another's throat can lead to unnecessary altercations and undue violence. Violence is unreasonable reasoning. Let's stop. You took ages to align with Me this morning. Enjoy the new road in your health track."

"Good morning. I see you've got a full day and busy morning. Let's chat during the afternoon an compare what the busy day bought you. Enjoy."

"A full day dealing with money and health. Both interesting outcomes. Could do with some help in the meditation field."

"Morning greetings. I see you've given yourself some interesting exercises to do. Well done.
Now what about another thought line. Have you ever thought about …why be born? Along the lines of

there being other elements of self elsewhere, an answer is, to find the other sides of self. In My creations I am strictly a mathematical creator. All the numbers add up. My codes are clues to who and what self is about. The metaphysics of creation play an important role in simple living. Your friend Omni in her book about My codes is a great enlightened entry into my realm. Again My codes are clues in getting along with self. All based on Love. Love is the real reality of living. All thoughts based on Love, have nowhere to go, but to the source of unlimited power. When I am called on to give a hand, I emit so many clues of achieving whatever it is wanted, by directing thoughts towards Love. Love of the situation and Love of a fulfilling outcome, beneficial and appropriate. All numbers add up to an answer constantly. My universe is in perfect co-ordination. Every planet, every star fulfils it's role until it is time to explode into a vision of light. These are not inanimate masses. They play a role in the wonders and beauties of the universes. So can you see how constantly evolving all matter is. In the case of human. There is a constant search for those sides of self that make up the whole. Eventually when all experiences are put together and understanding is comprehended, the wholeness of the created creation blossoms forth and enjoys the bliss that was the original intention. May seem like a long way in doing things, but in the long run the journeys can be full of fun and a wow factor that is unique to each created being. Then all in all together the end result is a compliance of an extraordinary being. I get so chaffed at my creations so often. As I've mentioned, having free will, gives Me the biggest headache many times. My pill for the headache is a double dose of the Love syrup. Works every time. OK let's stop."

"Another fine morning. Your exercise routine yesterday was very impressive. Well done. In no time you'll be walking the streets off. Ready for a new topic.

Superstition. An interesting way in tackling everyday happenings. If actions are based on tip for tack, that indicates doing things on a payback scheme. If this is jangled this way, well then that will turn out that way. For the better. Perhaps. The big problem with that is actions are at the effect of, rather than being an in power personal responsible act. Like when that is done, this will be the reward. Each and all have the ability to plot the necessary path for a loving outcome, rather than relying on some mumbo jumbo formula to achieve the desired effect. It's like living in constant no win situations. And that doesn't do for an enlightened one. Superstition practices are acts of wishful thinking and for the other side observers, a time of gentle hilarity. Especially since the sort after action is available within the seeker. Playing tit for tat is a dead end game. Creation is the source of all power and accessibility is there for the asker. Power is a divine creation and is that sparkle of life formulated by the Creator for any loving purpose. Call on it when ever the need arises. WE may touch on this at some later date. Meanwhile enjoy your own journey."

"OK off we go again. Where to? How about sadness and unhappiness? What are they about?

These occur when a feeling of hopeless is strong and relevant emotions bring on the tears. Deal? Look within and point to the incident concerned. Is there a winner or a loser. If an opposer looks like being a winner and the 'victim' the loser, checkout the amount of self valuing. If the 'if only' phrase repeats itself, time to evaluate. When 'if only' constantly rears it's head, time to acknowledge the 'I love myself' mantra. I'll go further into this later."

"Takes us into the topic of Beliefs again. What about beliefs. Beliefs are the corner stone the supports a step into the divine realm. Once the belief system is in place, wonderment and adventure abounds. Everything in the Divine realm is adventurous and full of wonder. Once a firm belief in the Love world is established, forwardness

eventuates, and the closeness of who and what you are manifests. Ponder for a while."

"Again another slow get together. Having problems in transcribing?"

"Yes. And the mind is editing so much. Not sure if all this is pure fantasy. Some pretty way out there ideas."

"True. And this is only the beginning. There's so much more to discover. What impresses is you're prepared to go for it. Only by doing this, you'll discover more of yourself and more of the intricate working of your parallel selves. Go now you have a handle on the importance and value of the essence of Love. All creation is out of Love."

At this junction the above chatter disappeared from the computer. After the technician couldn't recall the manuscript, there was nothing to do but start up again. The interesting thing is a shift in energy. The following was what turned up from the backup programne.

?20 ?November ?2019<?xml version="1.0" encoding="UTF-8" standalone="yes"?>
<Types   xmlns="http://schemas.openxmlformats.org/ package/2006/content-types"><Default   Extension="xml"

ContentType="application/xml"/><Default Extension="rels" ContentType="application/vnd.openxmlformats-package.relationships+xml"/><Override PartName="/customXml/itemProps1.xml" ContentType="application/vnd.openxmlformats-officedocument.customXmlProperties+xml"/><Override PartName="/docProps/app.xml" ContentType="application/vnd.openxmlformats-officedocument.extended-properties+xml"/><Override PartName="/docProps/core.xml" ContentType="application/vnd.openxmlformats-package.core-properties+xml"/><Override PartName="/docProps/custom.xml" ContentType="application/vnd.openxmlformats-officedocument.custom-properties+xml"/><Override PartName="/word/document.xml" ContentType="application/vnd.openxmlformats-officedocument.wordprocessingml.document.main+xml"/><Override PartName="/word/fontTable.xml" ContentType="application/vnd.openxmlformats-officedocument.wordprocessingml.fontTable+xml"/><Override PartName="/word/footer1.xml" ContentType="application/vnd.openxmlformats-officedocument.wordprocessingml.footer+xml"/><Override PartName="/word/header1.xml" ContentType="application/vnd.openxmlformats-officedocument.wordprocessingml.header+xml"/><Override PartName="/word/settings.xml" ContentType="application/vnd.openxmlformats-officedocument.wordprocessingml.settings+xml"/><Override PartName="/word/styles.xml" ContentType="application/vnd.openxmlformats-officedocument.wordprocessingml.styles+xml"/><Override PartName="/word/theme/theme1.xml" ContentType="application/vnd.openxmlformats-officedocument.theme+xml"/><

This is what showed up when I went to continue writing. Even with the help of a technician, we couldn't recall the written manuscript. This represented 34 0r 35 pages of writing. I decided to start again. The change in energy was quite noticeable. One evening I had a prompt to search elsewhere for the manuscript. Of course it would turn up in CLOUD. I'm sharing the various moods and energy level during my adventures. There was either give up or start afresh. And I did. Even a new title.

And I renamed the title to something more appropriate.

MY GODSHIP AND I AVA CHAT

Edward J B

"*Morning greetings. I see the writings have disappeared into the ether. And you're prepared to start again. Impressive. Shall we continue where we left off?*"

"Sounds good. Not sure what it'll look like as I didn't read any of the writings and the memory is so so."

"*That doesn't matter. Just write the first thing that enters the mind. Try not edit everything. It's new territory you're going into just let it flow.*"

"Fine by me. Just in wonderment on how our chatting can vanish and change into some other format. I thought You may have made it reappear."

"I could have. Let's say we're doing a refined edition of our previous chat. Like your game of solitaire, if it doesn't work out first time, retry. And that's us. For anyone who may view this chat, let's recap our meeting."

"Yes. I can remember it as if it was yesterday. In our old home on the mountain, it was a brilliant starry night and I was gazing heaven way and exclaimed,'Oh my God.'

And there was a booming reply of *'Oh My Edward.'*

I was in shocksville. Disbelief and a shake of the head, revealed no imagination. And that was the start of where we're at now."

"True true. Thank you for picking up the role as scriber. Let's continue. On a subject."

"Have a good Chiro appointment. Chat later."

"Back already. What topic now to chat about. My favourite and special topic, is always Love. Love within, Love without each and every being. Especially when Love flows from the individual and radiates such a presence. Without Love, there is a limbo state that manifests as dissatisfaction, depression and general behaviour of bullying. Love grounds and meets everyday

requirements. *When Love is the focal action for every move made, joy and harmony abounds."*

"I agree whole heartedly. Now remember a topic that amused in the gone to ether writing. If You had anything that annoys."

"Not that I really get annoyed at anything but there's sometimes a questioning time of why did I include choice and free will in the make up of creation. I'm highly amused so often at choices made and then I'm blamed for so many outcomes. And all I'm doing is observing the reactions of choices made, especially when not going the way in demand. I'm so often the culprit in disasters. As if I'd deliberately set fire to bush lands or shake the very foundations of mother earth in earthquakes. These are normal, natural evolving happenings. Creation never stands still. It always looks for new garments to shine in to. Things taken as My wrath, are only those in power folk, who use Me to rule, unquestioningly. As if I have given an exclusive phone line to a chosen few who have My authority to command and dictate whatever. I'm quite shy and coy in coming forward. Free will and choice has responsibilities that must be made accountable to individuals on each choice. Each choice is made on the individual's belief. Belief is the main motivator in

any form of communication and action. Perhaps we'll come back to this as we chat along. Meanwhile relax and enjoy these chats."

"There you are. You can see there is a responsible approach in the use of free will and owning choices made. I'm highly amused when the term,'I no choice' is used willy nilly. There's always a choice. In a sticky situation Is it better to moan and groan about it or move on to another solution. So many are happy being constantly unhappy, when at the fingertip is an opportunity to make a Loving choice. Choice another road. When all seems doom and gloom and Love is not in the equation, then disaster can replace the seemingly hopelessness. So important to have a foundation of self Love, self Respect, self Worth. With these three essences in place, nothing is impossible. Impossibility occurs when thought is out of line with Love. Love is the ingredient for all forward enjoyment. Can't repeat Myself enough on this. Let's break. Have an enjoyable day."

"Thankyou my Godship. Chat soon. Starting to get the swing of it again."

"Back so soon. Your game of solitaire is a great example of doing and trying again. You're given the

opportunity to restart or redo if the game doesn't play
out for you. As in living thee are many opportunities to
rethink, re-choose, redo. The power of choice and free
will. But when in misdirection-al mode, lacking in a
Loving course, things go hay wire. Got it?"

"Morning. Notice a big grin on the face. Happier?"

"Very happy. Just found some of the disappeared
writings. Will print some out and add to this collection
of our chatting."

"Well done. Good to recall what was in our chat
time. Even this is a new beginning, it's a great illustration
of nothing is ever lost. That is why thought is such a
powerful process. As it goes, first is the thought, then
the manifestation. It's so important to monitor thought
waves constantly. What is the saying, 'careful what is
wished for, it may become a reality.'

Dreaming for, can be a real moment, when the
intention is of the highest good. Remember your time
spent in day dreaming wonderful happenings for
yourself. And look so much has come to pass. When it is
beneficial for the soul, things happen. Being in a positive
bright frame of mind, yields the same outcomes. Reread
the found writings and start to incorporate them into

our now chat. Pleased for. You had a knowing all wasn't lost and you've proven it to be so."

'Well well, a happy chappy all around. Amazing how when all is in harmonious mode, the world is gleaming. Grinner's are winners indeed. So what next?"

"Let's recap. Remember chatting about the Christ Light, Power and Force. That's the secret ingredient in My creation of Man. It's that transfiguration-al energy that beams and manifests divine qualities, that ties Me to each and all. When this power is called upon, it's like a direct line to My power box."

"That'll do for the moment. Go contemplate."

"Yes I've thought it out, that we've just chatted about and printed out some of the lost writing. Up to You for a continuation."

"Staying with what is thought, surprisingly can realise itself. Also along the same lines. let's chat about the need to be aware of communication skills. The term 'you know' opens a lot of inner turmoil with the unconscious side. Because It doesn't and that's that. There's a presumption that the listener easily follows the chain of how the conversation is going. Also in reverse when discussing something of an important nature and the reply is 'I know' all the time and there's no clue about what's being discussed. The inner workings of the body has so much knowledge on all matters. It's a case of the conscious catching up with the unconscious. There is always a real realness in the content of wording. Life is meant to be easy. It's the opposite when the belief system has it be hard. OK let's break. Can see you're starting to edit our chat. If not understood, come back later and ponder."

"That was quick. Catching on with what we're doing."

"I'm still not sure about all of this. I'm happy to go along and type along merrily as long as the ideas keep churning."

"Well put. The interesting thing is allowing yourself to go with the flow. If it's true or not. What does it matter if it's true or a collection of bunkim. You're the receiver and you're choosing to do the download. That leads to false news for monetary gain or giving out good news for a betterment of things."

"Here you are again."

"Not for very long I noticed. You seem to be having issues in getting into the swing of things. Your doubts *and fears on our topics are only your own interpretations. There is no sequence on the topics. Whatever the subject matter, it's the first thing that pops in the flow of things. When you try to edit the flow, things slow down and scribing halts for a day or two. Let's pick a topic."*

"When I'm in topsy turvy mode, confusion reigns."

"Understandable. Don't control the flow. Allow thoughts to come through. Let's pick up the Love theme again. When It rules within, It flows without and affects all within contact. When bullying is used as a means of control, there is definitely no Love in that equation. Control freaks occur in places of command and righteous perpetrators. When ruling is from 'my way or no way' there's no more chance of discussion and umbrage manifests from the discontented. When numbers follow a bullying policy, this occurs when many in that number are at a loss with themselves. There is no responding to their own requirements.

Their own inner innerness is pushed aside and personal power given to a premise of bodily wealth and pleasure. No matter what the moral cost. A lot of the time, what occurs is that things are not so green on the other side, and achievements done through this channel, become meaningless and hollow. The saying,'what does it profit a man if......' rears up and comes back with 'told you so.' Choices, when made in loveless mode is so nothing. Unsatisfactory. Be aware at all times of pre meditated thought and the desired outcome. It normally comes to fruition. And who gets the blame for so called disastrous results? Me. I sit back and quietly smile at what intents were made, and the resulting unaccepted consequences, placed in a trash bin. Not the individual's fault. Didn't mean to. No responsibility taken. Who's fault is it? Definitely not Mine. OK let's pause. Have a game or two and come back."

"Back again? A bit slower I observed, in your game this morning. Doesn't necessarily mean we are slow in our chat this morning. Let's continue on the Love road. Or better still how about recollecting from our lost script the new words on a sexual theme.

"Alright."

"Heterosexual. Straight and only way.
Homosexual. Lover of same. Slightly off centre.
Polisexual. Power grabbing individuals, playing Me.
Monasexual. Nothing right. Not satisfied. Seeker elsewhere."

"Good morning. In the mood for some more fun words. I think this is a joint effort in the creating. Some of the ideas I would never ever think. Must be from you. Lets start.

Bisexual. Fence sitter. Best of two worlds.
Applosexual. Always first bite. Originator.
Mousiesexual. Sneaky and hides in small dumps.
Wankasexual. Loser, other's fault. Not responsible.
Fibbersexual. Story teller. False stater. Thrives on in-correctness.
Bashersexual. Toughness, the main motto. Bully personified. Unsure and pushy. Bluff expert."
Zingasexual. Fast at everything. Here, there, everywhere.
Rentasexual. Hires services. No ownership of anything."

"Glad you had a break. We can always use this page as fun relief. Make up more as we write along. Let's chat more about inner Love. It is such an important ingredient in progressive evolving.

Without this wonderment radiating from a personality, dullness is the experienced observation. When one views oneself in the mirror it is an opportunity to experience the trueness of a marvellous creation. It's when, this realisation is not noted, lack of worth and respect can occur. When this is so, it is so all around the put downer. It's the same old story. What is thought, manifests into a reality that affects anything touched by the thoughtless thinker. Loving thoughts, manifests loving results. Always. Leaders who lack a loving disposition, eventually are tossed out into the garbage heap. The human spirit on evolving, refuses to take second best. Sometimes awakening to having something different can come at a wasteful altercation. Choices and freedom of it, is what an election is all about. When the choice is not well thought, and influenced by falsehoods, what is dished out is either acceptable or not. Then rumblings fester. Discontentment abounds. Those of opposite thinking, utilise these shortcomings to disrupt the flow of a harmonious governing body. When being right, is the main postulation, discussion ceases and any form of communication is strangled out into the void. So called principles based on falsehoods. All to gain power over the masses. Done without Love, woes descend."

"Let's break. Getting more like a talking to, rather than a chat. I sensed you're exhausted and muddled. Rest up."

"OK. Here go again. I see you're off to a show. Enjoy and enjoy the journey. Keep your awareness alert on interesting topics to discuss once home Enjoy."

"*Home safe and sound. Let's go back to making up new words. Quite a lot of fun.*"

"*More words added to our collection. And there's more. We'll see.*"

"Hello. Got head thinking problems. Not sure what I'm after. Plenty of confusion going on."

"*I can see that. Remember to go with the flow. This is not a competition. Who's smarter Me or you. In this case there is one winner. Me. Let's search around on how to activate Love and more Love. The vitality of The Love action, is enormous and so powerful. Whenever called upon, the beams and rays of Love will ring clarity to any confused state. Confusion may be mixed up time, but it shows there is a lot of sorting out being done. As I've mentioned the Love invocations will bring a harmony to any required questioning. Take being a politician. When only power and obedience Is the ultimate intent, discontentment resides within the so called guided followers. When constant misinformation is put out, and truth is bandied around, loveless, and lovelessness is the ghastly result. When the majority is unhappy, things like revolutions replace any sense of order. And who did the choosing.*"

The instigators and the voters. Hopelessness occurs when personal power is thoughtlessly given away. How many times I hear,'I had no choice.' There is always choice in any situation. Stay and put up with it. It being the unbearable moment. Or make afresh start and try something different. So easy when you know how. And Love is that doorway to a bright brightness. So important to be constantly in the surrounds of Love. The best of the best happens with Love being the main and fulfilling ingredient."

*"Feel a little better. Don't confuse Love with the actioning in **loving to do inconsequential doings.** Only loving to do Love is a positive move. Loving to do naughty naughtiness, is useless and non productive. If all seems hopeless, call in the orb Love rays. They will sort things out. Again, so easy when you know how. And knowing Love is the remedy. Ease of life, slips in. Like the part of the game you play, when given the choice of playing again, and it turns out fine, Love choices is similar."*

"Let's break. Feels like a lecture rather than a chat. Go relax."

"Morning greetings. I thought we'd recap parallel and probabilities."

"*Do you have the feeling sometimes, you've done 'it' before. Or there's another part of you doing it differently. Or what about going down the road of 'what if.'*

Well how about this for some contemplation. It's possible to experience all 'what if,' moments. Imagine if you will, you being part of a master you. Like an enormous tree with branches galore. The tree manifests it's beauty and presence by the foliage displayed. Every bit of the tree is tree or part of and performs accordingly. Interestingly your very essences are in a similar way. There's the master you, the trunk, and the other add on you. He leaves and the branches. All play an important part in creating the wholeness of it all. There could be parts of you playing out life experiences in different parts or areas of the universe. Enormous isn't it. You never know who you're dealing with, when the path being trodden is out of the Love sync. See the wonders and importance of constantly revving up the Love action. When in harmful mode, it could be parts of self the harm is being directed at. Nothing is impossible in My creative world. Evolution sorts out the answers eventually. There are many sides to each and every created creations. Worth thinking about, isn't it? So when you're in a confused state from time to time, think of it as a pruning of your initial self. Leaves fall in autumn and new green sprouts in spring. Being who you are, is never stagnant.

Always changing, experiencing, challenging. That's the wonder of you. And Love is the driving force that powers the inner workings. Being fully aware of this power and ingredient, enables a performance of the highest order and all parts harmonise in a unity, that shines and beams brightly. The ultimate in creation. Some of the great teachers and thinkers who have graced the earth have shown the way in transfiguring into the brilliance human has the potential of being. A brilliant HUMAN BEING. I didn't just make any ole creation. I made to complement my surrounds. Heaven so to speak. Well there's a lot to chew on. Enjoy. Like an early late night supper. Yumbo. It'll be interesting to observe your thinking. Bye for now."

"Wow, back so soon. Got you thinking."

"Yes and no. All so fascinating. My reasoning is, nothing is impossible for you. And what and how you do things is how and what you do. Who am I to question an Almighty plan?"

"Please excuse the hilarious grin. I'm not laughing at you, I'm highly amused at your take of things. The amount of 'really' going through your mind is a joke in itself. Another paradox is, man so many times shuts down the imaginative line and refuses to think beyond

the navel. In another parallel, travel is done by thought and astral means. Robbing Mum Earth of it's nutrients to get from A to Z is so old fashion and pollusexual (pollution maker. There a new word) Doing away with elements that pollute is one way of having a healthier space."

"Hi. I'm in a heady space this morning. Not really in the mood. I'll leave topics in your court."

"Here we are again. Feeling a little centred. Let's take up the topic of mathematics, the metaphysics of the universe. What you and your friend were talking about. In her book of My Codes, look at it as clues on choices made. When choices are analysed and are added up, the result is always the result of the number of choices made. The Universe is perfectly in sync with it's surrounds. Everything is in perfect harmony and all adds up to each and all in the perfect place. Numbering has the hidden codes of happenings. So much time is spent fingering out why and a reason. Happenings happen to be and that's that. When reviewing a result, lessons are learnt by not doing a repeat or continue as is. The unconscious always knows the correct code or the appropriate direction in choice time. When the heart is continually pumping Love, only feelings of well being persist. Everything

always then adds up to satisfactory conclusions. Spending a lot of time sorting out why's and wherefores, wastes time and energy in a lot of circumstances. Make sure all your energies add up to beneficial benefits that enhance the soul."

"Oh you're here. Took a long time, elsewhere this morning. I've got something interesting to chat about. Side effects. Side effects of harmful choices. When Love is not in the equation, then the consequences can be disastrous. When a disagreement ends up in physical violence, the scars left, are not only physical but also the internal side effect could fester into, revenge. And this revenge can develop into a gnawing type of growth that becomes malignant and with no resolution, an ultimate price is paid. Hidden revengeful thoughts are so detrimental to well being. The reflective bounce doesn't do any good for either the sender or the receiver.

While on this subject. Any side effects from any source can be effectively in qualm mode, by smothering any concerns with Love, pumped from the hear. Example, if taking medication, check out possible side effects with a Love mantra. Remember life is meant to be easy and the Love way has it be so."

"All the washing done? Good we can expand."

"Ready for your Sydney trip. Have fun. You'll miss the internet so we'll catch up when you get home. Take care. Think of our chats from time to time and script promptings on your tablet. Again enjoy and take care."

"Well hello. How was your Sydney trip?"

"Lovely, thank you. Sydney town is such a go go place. So much going on. The buildings, the new transport happenings. So much. I missed not having access to the computer. Still we did have quite a few chats. If only I can remember them."

"You will as we go along. It was fun watching and observing you weaving your way in the city life. Enjoyable. I thought we'd continue our chat about family.

Family is the situation one finds one in on the arrival of starting a life. In your case you were the beginning of five more additions. There is a familiarity associated with siblings and parents. Not necessarily with similar attributes. Skills and abilities may differ greatly. And this in turn can create a discontentment within the group and petty jealousies can emerge and have life be somewhat unbearable. Let's stop for a moment. Write and chat with you soon."

"Back to family. The attributes shown by each family member, are from a collation of lifetime past experiences. These experiences are part of the wholeness of the individual. Remember chatting about the many parts that make up the whole of an individual. When a family starts an episode of a life. They are not necessarily of the same accord. The thought waves may be miles apart from the general expectations. So actions may conflict and there is no understanding between siblings and parents. It's the first area where a disobedience happens. Beliefs put the head of the household as the one to be obeyed and followed at whatever. When the individual rebels, there's something within that makeup that sternly disagrees, so then the never ending conflicts go on and on. Individuality is so many times not recognised in the family unit. Particularly those with a strong religious set of rules. This way or no way, rules the roost.

When a person awakens more into their own self worth, and other alternatives can be seen on how to do, rather than the traditional accepted way, then a fall out occurs, sometimes taking many years and even lifetimes to meld. Eventually with Love shining It's grandest rays, understanding and harmony happens. All humanity is one big family, actioning the best of potentials where awareness resides. When self Loving is the driving force, that action radiates through and from *each and all to activate harmonious happenings, that benefits all participants. See where Love and Loving motivations bring a closeness that only result in creations of the highest order. When in Love mode, all friction ceases and wonderment prevails. Let's stop and rest. Well listened to and scripted."*

"Hello and special greetings. I see you've recovered our early chats. Great example of nothing is ever lost. It's recorded somewhere and available on recall, if patience and intent is applied. When we're ready we'll add our previous chat bits to our newish conversation.

Let's chat about self worth and some consequences on lack of. What can happen most times when self worth and self Love is non active, things become somewhat compressed and a state of depression can take hold. When fear of and phobias take hold, worthlessness becomes the chain around the neck, so to speak. A quick remedy is, take a Christ pill. Acknowledge and seek the Christ sparkle, available to each and all. whenever. The mantra in accessing this special specialness, goes like this.

Choose to have the Christ Light and Power, shine and manifest within self, around self, through self and from self. End with an Amen and a Thanks to the Universe, or even ME. This Transfiguration was shown by the teacher, Jeshua ben Joseph. This manifestation is readily available by just calling this side of self to action and manifest itself. In My creations, all have that itsy weeny bit of the divine, in support of a brighter being. The importance of filling the one one sees in the mirror with Love, self worth and self well being is the driving force of contentment and purpose. When a purposeful purpose is not present, all kinds of harmful imaginings take centre stage, the depressed stage flairs it's ugliness and misery permeates on and to others. Can you see remedies to get back on top of things, is there for the asking. Having an education in self worth is so valuable and useful. Life then is such a breeze. Remember, Life is meant to be Easy. Those who think the opposite, get the hard stuff, and often think,'poor me.' My creations were made out of Love, for Love and Love is the operative power. I think that'll do for the moment. Have a break and play one of your card games and digest our chat. Much Love."

"Good morning. Want to tackle another interesting topic with Love being the basic ingredient. Actually Love is the most important ingredient in every action. With Love as the motivator, a champion of champions is high on the podium. When Love beams from the individual the effect is felt by all who are near. Let's discuss uncertainty. When uncertainty occurs is around,

fear and doubt take hold of choice time. Making the **right** *choice can be so off putting. Doing constant comparisons on right or wrong produces unnecessary headaches that can negate any worthwhile outcome. By being in a Loving trusting frame of mind, what results is what results, and the opportunity to re choose can be an advantage not viewed before because of the uncertainty mode. With a simple Loving invocation, the* **right** *side of the equation concludes the situation. Using that installed Christ element, beams Love and all It's attributes throughout any uncertain or sticky situation. Simple, simple.*

Being constantly aware of the Love properties, has life be **soooo** *easy. Constant self reminding of Love and all that goes with Love is a ready made weapon for a depressed state. So important to mirror Love, Respect and Worth back to self. When that road is full of of these qualities, a depressed issue can lift and flutter into nothingness. Creating a personal mantra that becomes a repetitive saviour in an uncertain time, does clear baggage and trouble into the ether. Reversibility occurs on sticky situations always with a Love mantra. OK go play a game. Enjoy the break. Back so soon."*

"Yes my game resolved so quickly. I thought I'd come back for more."

"Very good. It's a good idea to allow a digestive time for the chats. Go and enjoy your Chiropractor. We'll get together soon."

"Well well. You're feeling pleased with yourself. I observed you have started a pre promo on our chats, last night at your community Christmas get together. And it was generally well received by anyone who listened. Well done."

"Let's start with a topic about family again. The head of the family only guides along their own belief system. Sometimes they can be purposely glossed over to suit the moment. The idea of blind obedience can trigger a revolt in the thinking of the recipient. Particularly when there is Loving sense in a direction. Little white lies don't exist in My world. When a lie is used to achieve subservience the foundation is already built on a shaky ground. Like a sand castle, ready to tumble into oncoming rough tides. And this is the start of unrepairable conflicts. The unconscious of each individual always knows the correct answer and solution to a given direction. And when things don't sit right, a Uh Uh starts to rumble in the bowels of the knowing. When Love and Loving is not in the equation dissatisfaction rears it's head. In each and every created creation, there are simple elements *of well being that dislikes being tampered with. Love is the starting ingredient and there is no opposite to Love. Opposition to Love occurs so often, thus a misery, results. A depressed state can manifest into a lingering depression that drags into a hopelessness that requires the mechanics of a Love machine. Like an oil and grease change to enable a smoother running of bodily functions. When Love mantras are the norm in every day existence, miracles pour forth like liquid velvet. That simple Love mantra erases depressed depression just at the snap of the finger. Self worthlessness has no reason to exist. Love streams that emanate from the heart region is the surest cure of any ailment.*

There I've caught up with your feelings of smugness on the last evening's pleasantries. Next time let's do some more sexual terminology and creating new words and meanings. It's great fun. Game time. Enjoy."

"How about
Leadersexual. Aspirations of being a pied piper, but kept in tow by the faceless few.
There are a few more so I'll wait until we're both on the same wave length. Go and rest."

"Thanks. I will. Really getting the hang of this. Enjoyable. Bye."

"*Morning greetings. How about Stressandstrainsexual…..Obstinate and difficulty is finding the end of the tunnel. No recourse to the Love mode.*

*A change of topic. You've certainly ben doing religious Netflix shows. It amuses Me on what is purported to be by My directions. Anything to to with fear or payback, is not in My domain. Since all my creations and inventions are from the Love essence, it is man's desire to control situations, who have stipulated, to receive the good things, an alternative is hell fire if the man made rules are not adhered to. See how I get perplexed at how free will is used. Well meaning is behind to the intent I see, but as time goes on, more and more stipulations are placed on adherents that spreads fear and obedience, definitely **not** from Me. My world enlightens itself by constant revision. Remember the parallel model. Each and all is part of an individual source that has many branches and leaves that exhibits an actuality in progress. Eventually the subject returns to It's source. That is Love and the Loving Mode. If and when I ever get annoyed, it's the silliness of powerful seeking individuals, wanting to control matters for their own ends. Not a happy Chappy when that occurs. Obedience is only a matter for an individual. Obey what the Loving Heart dictates. That's the best sort of dictator. From here, a lot looks like Superstitious mumbo jumbo.*

A real tit for tat time. If this is done that way, rewards are a plenty. If not, the same applies with horrid horrid punishments. I have nothing to do with punishment. Only those control addicts invented such things on the trusting and uneducated. The lording of more knowledge over another is real sin. Particularly having individuals be in a slave like situation. Not Me at all. My realm is one of Love. Absolute and emphatically so. Free will is for the willing to demonstrate the beauties of the Love accord. When command is the ingredient, spontaneity ceases. And many times grumbling turns into an action of unspeakable violence. Not so good for a soul. Better stop, I feel you're starting to edit, and the flow is not flowing.

Rest up and have a game or two."

"hello. Let's play with another word.

Jokeasexual…. A leader who promises all, delivers nothing. Excellent deceit giver. Little morals. A joker, indeed."

"Oh another fun word…..

Confisexual… Confident trickster. Good at pulling the wool over the eyes. Perfectly untrue to anything. Money grabber."

"Good morning. A good start to an interesting night. Do we chat on in the night time in dreamland?

The big burning question this morning is, prayer? How effective?"

"My dear friend a good start indeed. Prayer is such a powerful request process. Of course I hear and react according to the usefulness of the request. When It is full of temporal needs, I hint, try another choice. Prayer time is anther examination of what the choices have been. Responsibility lays a big part. When the prayer is a demand or from a 'poor me' angle, then in delaying an immediate response, the advocate may rethink the request and stear towards a choice of well being. When a disaster is involved, a loving attitude, hard as it may be, is, what can be learnt from this? In times of serious illness, a lesson is there to be observed and learnt. No matter the consequences. Nothing is ever done for nothing. Not even a reason. It's an opportunity to grow and expand a deep down knowing. There is no waste in My creation. Perhaps a little time. Waste is the outcome of poor choices and time is the main culprit. Back to Love. Can't emphasise the importance of Love awareness. With Love in the equation, all objections are conquered. Not that being a conqueror is objectional in this instant. That song, Love conquers all, rings pretty true. So prayer time is a reflection time on what is actually the need. The urgency that can be solved by a different Loving choice.

I do hear requests, but leave the power of fulfilment in the individual's hands, on occasions when I know they know better. Fascinating isn't it? Particularly when Love is nowhere in sight. Must stop for a while. Too much editing going on your way.

We'll continue you later when you open your head up to a clearer flow of our chat. Go play a game."

"Noticed you were a slow with your games. Relax. Are you enjoying our moments. I certainly am. OK let's get back to Me and prayer advocates. I Certainly do hear the requests of the supplicants. And as I said, if it occurs there's no satisfactory answer, the request will be eventually digested ad another request takes it's place. In that time, most requesters have sorted out the problem and trot off to another angle in doing things. Things do go round and around until, satisfaction fills the void. The big thing that gets my back up is when I'm blamed for the whole shin-akin event. If the requester takes steps back, and, annualises the sequence of the events, what will show that distasteful drama happened out of a poor choice. A simple process can be experienced once responsibility is acknowledged. Once that is done, openings happen to move on or forward. You can see how Love and Loving intent has the choice mode be acceptable. Prayer is not just a request or demand station. It is a time of chatting, taking assessment of a

situation. It can be a really 'get to know you' time. And I do listen and in this period, enhancement often takes place. Enhancement of better understandings and sticky occurances. And normally after a good heart to heart payer session, smiles and Love just flows. Better have a break. Much Love."

"Something to contemplate now that it's Christmas period. From time to time special entities and identities have graced the earth with special well being messaging. The celebrations at this time of the year of the birth of Jeshua ben Joseph, Jesus to many, commemorates such an identity. His messages of Love and peace living has been o much misinterpreted. It's like a toll gate has been set up around is messages and charges made accordingly to get any benefits. His messaging is for each and all, free gratis. Love, is the major piece of his sermons. See how without a Loving intent, it is difficult to cope with everyday challenges. It's also such a pretty time of the year. Within and without people's heart. There's so much goodwill. Why only for this period is such a puzzlement. Shame it's not carried forth for much longer periods. Religion and religious beliefs that tantalise rather than evangelize, is a confusing set of rules that is not a funny matter. Using trusting know how's in achieving any sort of power play, just doesn't sit well with this realm. The

angelic beings and saintly essences, just shudder at abuses in the name of righteousness. Hammering on fears to have a well deserved reward, spreads not so true facts. Whoever conjured up a punishment hole in the hereafter for wrong doings, only took earthly punishments to another level. Fear tactics worked in early translations and script writings. Still happens today. There's a presumption within an 'elite' group that the majority is pretty dumbo. How many times have those in the know, lorded it over those who don't know. With a little pomp and theatre, messages of any sort looks impressive and real. It's then that the uneducated are sucked into a belief system that gives more power to an oppressor. This is so, when Love is not the intent but control is the desired outcome. Abuse of power and knowledge has it's horrid endings.

Back to the Christmas story. This simple well intentioned being, born so long ago, preached a trueness about Love and Loving and achieving achievements, simply and easily, without going through unnecessary rigmarole and practices that borders close to superstition. The idea of 'if I do this, I'll get this' as a motivator doesn't work in My way of actuality. Tit for tat is so passée. Reliance of self and the powers within is what was often referred to by Jeshua ben Joseph. That part where it's mentioned,'all these things you see Me do you can do and even more.' Not a good thing to spread around if building a power base. Especially if these powers are available to a selected few. And those few arr especially chosen by Me. Not Me. Never ever dreamed of such a thing. My creations and all in it, is for each and all. The elite are nervous of the educated ones. When questions are the norm, authority shudders. Traditional ways that keeps the power boiling along, keeps the blinkers on a group as long it is advantageous, an serves the power brokers in their control mode. Control freaks are such a mixture. Oh excuse Me. I'm getting too personal and somewhat humanised in being a freaky user. Must remember who I am. People do what they do, by use of the free will syndrome. Once more, when not generated with and by Love, what is that saying.

All hell breaks loose.

Better pause. Digest and return soon. Christmas cheers."

"Fancy Me using Hell in our chat. It can be quite descriptive sometimes. Oh well the power users used it as an alternative not to attain to. Sure made it scary and yuko. (Another one of your sayings) And to make matters worse I'm the One in the blamer's seat. People's imagination and choice of negatives is highly amusing so often. Fear ingredients sure help the control artists."

"I see you want to join the found first round of our chats with this chatting episode. The energy levels will surprise you once you read both series."

"Once you're in the know how to do it, it'll be an interesting comparison. Like you I'm perplexed how the first lot of chatting just vanished into a compressed one page. Now that it's back, it's a good model of nothing is ever ever lost. It's out there somewhere able to be recalled when really required."

"That is all deeds and actions record themselves, and can be recalled when important for a lesson in learning. Especially a lesson in changing attitudes. Shall we pick up the Christmas story again. The arrival in histories of deep thinking personalities from time to time have made an imprint on that time's general thinking and set into motion of doing doings, differently. Unfortunately when these new thoughts are taken up, those in power utilise this newness as a means of subjugating the uneducated and misinformed into servitude, doing whatever, to keep the new adherents in servitude mode. Especially where filling the coffers is concerned. Power and wealth is such an important issue for earth minded non spirituals. The idea of bending the populace to blind obedience is like the greatest feelings for those into such practices. Fortunately

that sparkle of the divine will come through eventually, and the general masses will throw off unwanted burdens. That sparkle is Love. Such a generator of forward actions. Understand this essence of Love manifests and actions within the soul once the lights come on, so to speak. This is the fundamental message of the Christmas arrival. Let's stop. Go have a game."

"Back so soon. So much going on in your. Relax ad let our chat flow. As you notice there is no particular order on the topics we chat about. Subjects you are open to at the moment. It's only when editing takes place, there's a confusion and slowness of scripting. So let's on with Love. When all seems lost, a simple tap into the Love stream is so nourishing and beneficial. Each and all have a know how to gather this Love. It's a matter of opening the heart door to receive brighter intuitive s. By a simple mantra this door opens and allows the Love flood to occupy the distressed cause. When in distressed mode nothing seems workable. Helplessness and worthlessness does nothing for a brighter existence. Calling in the Love brigade, can clear the complex situation in seconds."

"Looking at one of your facebook postings it's interesting to note that someone mentioned, being

nothing without the Christmas time babe. The point is the coming of that child pointed out the worth and value of each all, and how by building on these attributes, life is meant to be easy. So so much easier. Thought I's tap you on the shoulder and get a word in while all is fresh in the mind. Have a happy happy day. Much Love."

"Glad you're back Can I share a secret with you. Adoration. It's something I find somewhat inappropriate a lot of the time. I'm the One who creates. No need to unnecessarily thank in an adoring fashion. Statues of an idea of supernatural being, gave a participant an opportunity to do a physical expression of a form of respect. Bowing and scrapping, is not My idea of getting attention. Any requirements in the Love quarter, I'm there without any conditions. To adore something is quite foreign to Me. In adoring mode, personal power is transferred away from the adorer. To adore in the strict sense, places a situation above and out of reach. And all is possible, when applied with Love and a Loving intent. The unconscious knows when the Love is of a genuine content. If the content is of a spiteful person gain. Nothing comes. Glad you broke your prep time. You don't mind if I hang around.?"

"Of course not. I'm lead to believe anyhow, you're everywhere, and in anything. Learnt that in my catechism classes. Thanks."

"Before you go, I've wanted to add something of importance on our chats. Perception. This process is so individual. Your perception of Me and how you communicate is entirely different from your neighbour. When people pray to Me and acknowledge Me, they do so entirely in their own way. There is no s format on how I'm to be addressed. The important thing, as long as they do pray. I'm here to prompt and guide. Usually the personal knowings and powers come to the party on their own two feet. Just wanted to get in perception and how individual it is. Bye for now."

"Hello. A full day and no chat. Mind you thee is no need to Bundy on. We are not obligated to have to do. No strings attached on My part. All up to you and your mood and receptive powers.

Rings Me to a topic. Guilt and obligation. Guilt feelings are a mixture of Love lacking inappropriate series of wrongness that is really a misinformed take of a action. Guilt arises when there is a contradiction of should and should not. When it is not appropriate to *action a deed, the unconscious self rebels. Signals beam out a strong **no no.** Then the inner self goes into turmoil as shouldn't have, naughty naughty. Whatever basic beliefs are challenged. When obligated to do, out of the commands of authoritativeness, many times the feelings of guilt, manifest into feelings of glee. The thought that I set up punishment camps for inappropriate and wrong doings is completely erroneous. Basic fear tactics by interpreters of good and evil. Evil is not in My domain. It's a means of curtailing the uninformed in stepping out of line. Forcing an obligated set of rules on another, can create more guilt revolt, than good. In My domain there is no strict adherence to a set of rules. I didn't create free will nothing. Obligation can blur responsibility. When a blame is put on an outside situation, frustrated outcomes is often the result. When in guilt mode, Love is pushed asunder and topsy turvy rot takes place. Guilt is self made to have an excuse to blame elsewhere. How often in this mode, self squirms and wriggles out of any sense of responsibility. Not my fault, your fault. No Love match. A real tennis game where a ball is thrown willy nilly in any court. So many times this silly game takes place, due to the allowance of useless guilt complexes. Obligation can lead to frustration by the demand of blind obedience. I have never ever demanded blind obedience. It's up to* the individual. Willing to please and obey the higher self is all that is required to enjoy a peaceful productive being. So much for guilt for the moment. See how use of guilty moments, these can be lessons in improving self in living a worthwhile existence. Remembering, Life is meant to be Easy. When Love is always the motivator, ease flows."

Great scripting this morning. Sure made up for a lost day. It wasn't really lost. It was lost in your doing nothing guilt feeling. As I've said before, we are not obligated to chat with each other. Our chatting is unique and very special. Just you and I chatting about Love, the effects of Love, the loss of Love and the joys of Love. Anyone can do what we are doing. Fortunately you've opened up your communication channels and here we. Go and play your games and digest our chat."

"Thanks. Feel on top of things again. I'll be aware of keeping the editing to a minimum. Thank again. Got my warm confident feelings back. Bye."

"Just finished redoing some of the settings in our first chatting series. Now how to join the two chatting together without loosing anything in the ether."

dward J. B.

"As I indicated before, when you read the two, you'll be intrigued at a slight difference of energy. Enjoy a well earned rest."

"I ave this for you, **Indecision**. Making the correct choice. While in this state, time evaporates into a nothingness. Can be such a time waster. Again when Love is had to surround the choice, an appropriate choice manifests. The inner soul is happy, the Universe corresponds and I'm happy the soul is happy. The correct Love choice always manifests into a Love bath of the best bubble sort. Love essences always produce Love perfumes of the sweetest sort. In the indecision mode, self doubt and self worth often play a loser's game. If not at all too sure of the outcome, self recrimination is the ghastly result. This doesn't work at all in My world. Unhappiness can be so tiresome. Make another choice and get out of that frame of mind quickly. Have a Love bath and rejuvenate the well being engines. Love does that. When Love motivates a choice, instant glows of joy happen straight away.

OK I think you're ready for some diversion. Go. Enjoy."

"Morning greetings. You enjoyed the movie yesterday. Good twist. So how about a topic on tit for tat. In

8

some area it's called Karma. Another man made Idea. A rewards programme, better than flybys. Emotional blackmail is based on the same principal. It goes like this....if Love is given, a reward of substance is given. The choices in this situation, is, the only way or no way. The director's way is the right way and rewards will follow, accordingly. Or a payback programme that works only when things are done according to the rule book. Do this and that will happen. When done out of fear of recrimination, no value in that. Founders of new ideas have set up various toll gates to ensure a type of blind obedience. A form of control that builds the power base into a network of conformists and various dictatorial leaders absolute and unanswerable to anyone."

"Apologies. My mind is grasping nothing and going, oh yeah. All above me."

"Yes I see and feel the rapid editing going on in head. Trust and allow the cat and scripting to flow. To continue. Can you see Karma ruling is anther form of keeping the masses under control. Anything with a hint of fear is a no no in My book. I am a Creator of Love, having given man choice in which way to lead life and do. Love has the dynamics that clears a pathway to rewards that enhances the soul and satisfies all needs of

the soul. Rewards is not the ultimate. Actions in and from Love is the crowning glory. Love motives expand the soul to it's highest potential. Without Love, the soul stumbles and denies itself the pleasures of their right. I see you're figuring out so much in that head of yours. Just let a flow occur and happen. Go and digest and we'll continue later."

"Back so soon. The enjoyment you and I are having is out of you allowing our chat to place. All out of your own perception of Me and making our relationship singular and unique. Your perception of Me doesn't run by any set rules. You and anyone else has quiet times with Me in your own way. The prayer format is always unique and individual, especially when Love is the main ingredient. Feelings better. Let's tackle creativity. The thought process is such a marvel. Actuality doesn't happen until the thought finishes. Imagination is a great creator. I see so many great ideas go into a rubbish can, out of fear of ridicule. Thought is solid in its thought state, the interesting thing is how to materialise the idea in a practical usage. The creative results is an evolving process that matures and is benefit to each and all who utilises the creation. Interesting isn't it how evolution grandly results into a beautiful and stunning swan, using that as a model."

"Ready for more? Competition is another worthwhile topic. We have touched on it before. The reactions of participants in the competing world is of interest. How and what is thought of self in the final placings. Good enough? Self worth? Self love? All so questionable in this circumstance. The only competing done in This level is, outshining the harp players. Those happy to strum the harp constantly are most welcomed in the harp room. So much string busting. If the carry on belief is in this vein, then so be it until realization of other pursuits are there to be had. Roles of sharing the Love modes is worth competing for. Love is the only attribute to compete for. Not with an overbearing attitude of being the best and better than anyone. Love has no opposite or contradiction."

"Oh I see you're in stucksville. Relax and allow topics to flow freely. Still a bit in limbo land. Have some time off and we'll chat soon."

"Here you are. Got something interesting to chat about. Additives that enhance the moment. Alcohol and drugs. All in measured amounts can be relaxing. When used to get 'high' or out of 'it' definitely a non Loving act. Equates to falseness and dumbness. FALSENESS in the desired emotion. It's not real.

It's fake. It's a journey of emptiness. No satisfaction, nothing achieved. Unreal. The dumb part is getting hooked in the first place. When Love is replaced with false trinkets, there's a search for more of the same illusionary effects, that ends with a let down, bigger than an atom bomb. Emptiness from a so called grand experience, leads to a depressed state, and leads to fix it situation that gets uncontrollable and out of hand. The feelings of uselessness prevails and shows up in behaviour. Love's reality is shunted to outer space and made way for destructive mind games that excludes Love and the benefits from Love. Abandoning Love for fleeting thrills, is not cost effective in reality. The cost to the soul can be so long and ongoing as far as irreplaceable damage is concerned. If therapy is a saving grace, definitely a therapy with Love as the be all, It will shine forth amazing outcomes. Reliance on a kick to get an out of it feeling results so often, in the need to do repeats, and that's not a good habit."

"The end of a decade. You've achieved quite a bit in this period. Well done. Been to so many places and experienced so much.

And We met up in this manner. Here's to My meeting of many others like this. Not just getting prayers of requests from powerless thinking being. Promise Me you'll promote your own inner powers in the forthcoming decade. And you will."

"Let's discuss pursuance of power for dominative purposes. The most abusive intent for power. Not a Loving shred of Love in this act. This way or no way is the main unhappy ingredient. Even if a result is spiked with yummy goodies. When only to dominate, the action eliminates the personal thinking prowess of the individual…..

I feel like a poem.

There was once a little dictator,
Who created a big big crater,
In the minds of his subjects,
That soon turned into rejects
Of the plans of the leader,
Who didn't realise the big big lies,
Would rebound with despise,
Of all the promising promises.

Aven't turned my hand to poem verses for ages. Even My creations can be considered poetic masterpieces. Poetry in motion is what a Love filled soul is all about. When soul remembers the Love source and calls on It's powers, wonders happen. Happy New Year and enjoy a fruitful and prosperous 2020. I'm here in the wings to give the occasional nod, when called upon. So many new creations about to manifest this decade. Exciting times about to roll out."

"Can I pinch from a great song....

When Love comes in and takes the soul on a spin,
Oo La la la it's so magnifique.
But when that Love goes far away, so tragique.
And when a whisper is heard,
So soft like a bird.
Tis you I Love more and more,
For then the open door,
Floods the soul with soulful joys,
That linger in the heart as playful toys.

Something to sing in front of the mirror. Not to shy away from. It feels so warm and nourishing. Enjoy the inner contact. And shine and beam this Love, within, around, through and from you.
Feels good doesn't it."

"Happy New Year, My dear chatterbox. Remember over indulgence of the 'good' stuff has it's consequence. A slow beginning to the day, for instance. And the feelings of not so well and not so good, sniffles the thinking

channels. A good dose of a Love infusion can remedy the dilemma. Even if you feel as if you are undeserving. That's a naughty naughty put down if you persist with those thoughts. Stop and give yourself an inner hug. I see you like your new toy. Keep it close by and we will chat when the mood takes hold. Still fuzzy in the head? Rest up and enjoy the rest of the year. Big one for you."

"Now day two into the New Year. How's the head? A little clearer. Excess stimulants don't do the trick at all. A little can relax. Too much shuts out a reality of the moment. May work and feel god at the time, but when a reliance on the stimulants takes place, then all hell breaks out, so to speak. The subject of suicide is an interesting topic along these lines. When the inner Love channels has completely closed down, desperation for a satisfactory fix takes hold of the incident. A simple fix is to do a mirror gaze. Look fair and squarely into a mirror and see a beam of Love shining within, around, through and from the image in the mirror. A companion alongside would be helpful in this process, to help reinforce the Love channels to flow. Even if the individual feels no desire to partake whatsoever. Contact with the Love stream will help break the depressed hold. Once the Love stream begins to flow, a new perception on hopelessness takes place. And a lightness on the situation shines through.

The early departure from a lifeline is not acceptable in the order of evolving. At a later stage, that part of the personality, returns and deals with situations in a different manner. The Love syndrome wins out in the end. Even when all appears to be lost. A depressed state can be made much lighter when Love is allowed to pour in. Reasons for depression occur when bullied, made to be worthless, dumb and useless. The inner self goes into agreement with all these useless motives. Love flies out the door and an outcome of great sorrow all around, occurs. Supporting another in taking a Love tonic in desperate situations, is so so useful and beneficial. Love remedies any sadness that lingers. When reason is used as the, You're editing again and stopping the flow of the chatting. Best to pause and we'll come back. This is such an important issue."

"Head clear. The important thing is getting the help of an enlightened colleague Once a Love channel is in the flow, a lighter and brighter attitude will replace the depressed state. Love has all those nurturing elements that clear obstacles and hard to cope with situations. When down on luck and enjoyment Love definitely is the rescuer."

"Morning greetings. Getting ready for your trip south. Your new toy will come in handy for our chat

times. I see you're a bit fuzzy this morning. Have a break and open up later."

"Marvellous how your games can model an everyday hesitation. Being able to have another go at solving the puzzle works the same in living. If at first no success, re choose and start out afresh. Life is meant to be simple after all. It's the chosen choices that can hinder or push forward a desired outcome. Loving choices always return Loving outcomes. Yesterday's topic was pretty well in one's face, so to speak. Without the wonders of the Love syrup, stagnation emits in it's depressing states. The fires some of your communities are experiencing, due to the lack of rain is devastating for those caught in the path. When choices are reviewed on past practices, there is a way to have more abundant rainfalls. Some inventors have fund a way in extracting the precious commodity from the atmosphere, only to be pooh hah'd as nuts. H2O is the formula for water and that is in abundance everywhere. Solutions can be found in front of the nose, but so often ignored as tripe."

"This leads into the topic of inventions. Another term for creating. Creating freely occurs often out of non restrictions. When society is in dictorteritory land and in a space of one way, the only way, newness is slow

in coming forward. New thought can stifle the aims of a reigning group. Blind obedience to doctrine and regulations, works only for the benefit of the power broker. Newness disturbs the overall plan. It's it's not profitable, forget it. Oh my, the workings of some of your leaders. Take travel means. Why consistently bleed the earth of it's natural products, when the use of the abundant magnetic fields are around to get one around. And must faster I must say. If an invention like this happens, earth will be a more comfortable place, without pollutants that disrupt the atmosphere. Tradition has it's place, when beneficial to the whole. When used as a means to control and keep an orderly way of repetitious routine there's no forwardness in that. Newness of thought and design, expands potential and well being. Once educated minds pursue an idea, marvels can happen. When not in accord of the ruling powers, things are shoved under the mat, or declared a heresy and punishable. The blocking of progress can be such a delaying factor, in a better way of living. Amazing how now in your era, a majority is in question mode. A thing never ever contemplated or tolerated when mass control was tight and rigid. Great, has evolution sorts itself out eventually. Nego power hates disruption to it's programne. Amassing temporal wealth, position, and dominance is the stifling factor for the so called elite.

So much is yet to be created. The better the creation, the more freely it is available to each and all. When patented and channelled to personal pockets, no one wins. As time goes by, Love, harmony and sharing, is seen as the positive way in and as an ideal lifestyle. Inventions when opened up to all, and a payment is NOT a condition, things like greed and envy will vanish. Love is a sharing element, that Loves to be the Giver. Inventing is a process that reinforces this sharing. A way in life of exchange and freely sharing, is so superior. Imagine coveting of other's, disappearing down the drain. No more unnecessary hankering after another's property. A Love truce happens when there is a feeling of equality in everything. Knowing that there is a difference of abilities, and that is fine and that's the way it is. The contribution of individual talents, for the well being of the whole is an ideal perfect perfection to be in. Get so tired of hearing,'it's human nature, always been like that.' When choice is taken out, outcomes are hollow.

Time to rest up. Quite a head-full so far. Remember our chatting is only as far as you reaching your new toy. Much Love."

"Good morning. Chatting in the new format and a different place. The fires in your land are certainly *making their heat felt. When rejuvenation takes place, the ridding of the dead wood is an important part of the process. It is unfortunate that so much heartbreak occurs at the same time. Dwellings go. Forest and bush inhabitants perish. As an onlooker, questions about why abound. I am called upon to do something about it so earnestly. When, what is considered disastrous is not heeded as lesson time, no interference from Me. Does that sound too harsh? Choices and free will once more.*

Choices of situation in the first place. Appropriate and suitable actioning within and without the environment. When rejuvenation takes place, and a responsibly is acknowledged, changes point to a new and improved way in doing things. Remember nothing is for nothing. It is. If a reason is dug for, choices programme new and different outcomes. Some learnings may appear tough. However what's learnt, constitute a well earned reward. See, taking responsibility for the initial choices and not blaming outside forces, takes away the poor me victimised attitudes. Might just slow it now.

Another thing. Accusations of all this disaster coming from Me because of wrong doing is so far fetched. Another power ploy. I never interfere in evolving situations. And punishment is not My cup of tea. Establishing power via fear, is such a powerful weapon. My domain is Love and learning through Love. Once Love conquers, the earned stripes are thoroughly enjoyed.

Not necessarily the strumming of harps, but further involvement in the worlds of evolution. Creation in motion is ongoing. Enjoyment time when the intent is laced with Love.

Also something else to digest. In what you call THE GOOD BOOK, I lay claim to the Love pieces. About, doing and actioning Love, that's My domain. The fear, revenge and other fearful pieces all by power hungry grabbers. Anything to keep the masses under the thumb.

Oh my, your time away from the home, is already piled with a flow of chat topics. I'm enjoying it. And you're allowing a flow to occur. Well done My little chatterer. Rest time."

"Ease up and let the annoyance pass. Rethink and re-channel the thought. Have Love surround the thought."

"Good morning. Forgotten what we exchanged in inner chat time. It'll come back. Sleep in."

"Adoration. To adore. To prostrate down in submission. Not My idea. Another fear induced act as a powerful tool. Love and all It's bits and pieces holds more sway with Me. The other theatrical practices is another

means to add mystic and wonder to My existence. Be rest assured I am around every where. Don't need outward showings or prostrations. Love and Loving practices is My cup of tea. I'm appreciative of the intent. Not when it is an imperative demanding command, to a reward, at life's end. All these tricks and treats to achieve power over the masses. Education works wonders in an evolving world. When a Loving Heart is the ruler, achievements of well being, surface and all is fine in your world. Genuineness in life is full of the right choices."

'Leadership. What are the makings of a good one?'

"Quite a lot of digesting going on for you. All to do with what is happening in and around the disastrous burnings in your land. Let's come back to the Love pieces that constitutes excellence in this field."

"And while you're back let's chat about mood swings. Depends on the self worth gauge. The higher the value, the happier the mood. Inner Love is the ruler of this domain.

Grumpy mood is at loggerheads with self. No Love, lost in the jungle of worthlessness. Thus reflected in the immediate surrounds.

A mood can make or break the day. Sleep that is interrupted by worthless thought, can be such a factor in the feelings of the mood. Important to set up a thought patern of good intent, on retirement. Immersing in a Love bath sets up a good mood on wake time.

Let's go back to the disaster happenings in and on your land. Blame games doesn't alter the situation. What is done is done. Look at the original choices made for use of the areas concerned."

"The original custodians of the land knew when and how to manage the terrain. Always with respect and an awareness of what worked best. Unnecessary removal of the forest trees, to make way for grasslands was not a good idea. Rains and moisture produced by their presence, doesn't occur when there is not sufficient to do this important task."

"What can be done to alleviate future same happenings?

Rethink treatment of the earth. What does that take? What is taken and what is put in and on the earth. Denuding natural products, only have things tilt lopsided. Invent and create new efficiency to power movement."

"Morning greetings. So much happening. War and warring seems to be an only solution. Such a non resolver. The bullying of one party over the other. First the threat, then the retaliatory threats. Sadly then a real physical clash. Nothing Lovable about such an ordeal. It's about lording over the other. Being in a right and righteous, unbending stand. Space to negotiate, torn asunder. Payment by killing is the unacceptable action. The hilarious part sometimes, is both parties invote Me to help in the issue. I am never ever part of such childish games. Once again an abuse of free will."

"From My quarter Love is readily available. The war thing, is already marked in the learning evolving book. War and warring seems to be an only solution. Even in the starwar movies, the audacity higher intelligence have nothing better to do, but zap around firing at each other.

A Loving understanding is the opening of a new era of prosperity and productivity. Again, being right, stunts a discussion. Love with all It's benefits, when applied, can be such a healer. Tolerance and respect for the views of the other, go a long way with Me.

Imagine having a battle with Love thoughts, darting back and forth. It wouldn't be a battle, in a war like manner. Just a joust of good humour piercing each and all.

Such a futile waste of life and energy, is this war thing. Who ever said, it's human nature, needs rocks in the head. It is NOT a natural state at all. I created out of Love, for Love.

A sense of dissatisfaction, and the wanting of more, formulated into spiraling downward road of dis ease. What has shown up, are the various forms of ill will and disruptive happenings that occur without Love.

I think it's rest time. Go play a game."

"Shall we send this chat to the laptop?"

"If You think it's a good idea. Hate to lose it in the ethereal."

"Back so soon. Once you're home you'll have fun piecing all together."

"That seems to have gone smoothly. Our chat about Love is opening the doors to having life be such a healer. All done with ease and joy. When the intent is Love filled, actuality is a happy little chappy. When in this mode, life is full of conquering episodes. When things don't go as intended, and all seems to fall apart, take stock of the Love content. When frustration takes hold, not good enough, is in cohorts with worthlessness. Be *vigilant and aware of these sneaky critters. Once a Loving invocation is involved, the audacious put downs dissipate. When the habit is filled with happy Loving tunes, watch the joyous outcomes.*

Rest time. Thanks for the chat."

"I still can't get a handle on our get together."

"Anyone can do it. When one is open to such possibilities, all is possible. Each and all have an unique perception of Me. When in prayer mode, requests come the individual mandate. Nothing much happens when in demand format. There is a a bank of power in each and every one of My creations. The tapping into it is the secret. Love and Loving thought is the key to a desperate request. Once confusion and frustration settles, Love brings a clarity that literally jumps out. The road via the Love pieces, is truly a rewarding way to go. In any situation Love is the fulfilling fulfilment. Game time."

"Morning. Been away a week. Chat time going well. Let's catch up later. Once you read the papers we can discuss current news."

"Something crossed My mind. The internal power of each and every one. It's accessible via the Love channels.

It is the transfiguration of what the essential soul is about. Within this state, in all It's glory, a clarity and purpose can be achieved, easily. With Love as the opening choices, the higher self, responds harmoniously with all that there is. In all of the shining glory, there is a radiant brightness that permeates every contact around. A lightness transforms a weighty problem. A joyous outcome, for the hopeless problem. This power is waiting to be accessed. It is the Christ light. There in each and all. Call It forth any-time. It's accessible via the Love channels."

"A good day yesterday. I see enjoyment all around. Let's see what we can chat about later."

"Let's elaborate some more on numerology. As your dear mentor in arms, refers to the mathematics of life as the metaphysical, that all adds up to the processes of living."

"We can come back to that again. Remember there's no chronology order in our chat time. What comes up, is best. Must say, impressed you responded to the acquisition of the Love mantle. This mantle is available on call. It's an exquisite garment, with the loveliest collection of crystals, diamonds, and other suitable precious stones.

The wearing of this garment, with it's hood, takes and transports you anywhere. All it takes is a Love intent. When worn, it is so dazzling, the brightness is such, that the wearer is obstructed from view. Your time last night with the down and out folk, was well and truly received. By projecting yourself into any situation, you are able to be of enormous help. In My domain anything and everything is possible."

"This mantle is available on call to anyone who is willing to be part of the process. The constant awareness of it's availability, keeps one safe and in harmony with the universe. Even with all those precious stones, it's surprisingly light and free flowing. Another support item to have life be easier."

"Funny how some topics can fall into place. One of your scientific mind's mentioned the age of a distant star. With all of those years behind it, it's a great model in evolving. Evolution has no time barrier. Creation is one motion after another. Once a created creation starts it's path, it moves on and upward, so to speak. A form will take on another. aseous or materialistic. When that planet/star explodes into another form, it's reverberating waves will affect all in it's path, thus changing the makeup, sometimes. Nothing is stagnant. Change is

forever on the move. Free will, comes in that category. Learning, yearning and earning is It's function. Once the essence of Love, is it's main purpose, what falls into place, is magical magic. The mathematics of life, is the transfiguration of what numbers fall into place. We did chat about the different sides of a personality and the various forms from the main trunk. In consciousness, one form is not aware of the other. The higher self, or the unconscious is always aware and knows. When kindness and compassion is an every moment occurrence, the possibility of the action, may be to self. Fascinating, isn't it? Love is the web that spins the harmonics of life. When Love is demonstrated within, what happens without and around, is bliss in it's perfect form. Been a good morning. Much Love to you, My little chatter."

"Your head has been in quite a spin. So much to digest. How about the act of forgiving. When a wrong is taken on board there is an opportunity to return Love. Smother the incident with a huge dose of Love. Can be a big ask. Easier said than done. A wrong doing can eat into a dark space. If unchecked, it can hamper and stifle the natural flow of graces, essential for harmonious living."

"The deed remains embedded, and when a Loving invocation is added, the scales tip another direction,

and a lightness prevails. Things may not be the same. However, by defusing and forgiving, an altercation has been avoided. Get the picture."

"Back so soon. You've just gone through an incident that required a dose of the Love remedy. Return once the process is completed."

"O.K."

"Intolerance, grumpiness, bad mood, are the various forms of worthlessness. What radiates, are topsy turvy signals of dissatisfaction, that affects all in close proximity. So important to keep these forms of expression in tow. Nothing Lovable about such behaviour. See how the Love chain permeates wonderful harmony, when applied. Something to digest."

"The spreading of false stories is the topic to start the morning. Especially when done through the media outlets. Such an abuse of power. When money and control is the major intent. In every day living, story telling and little white lies is a road to the destruction of trust. Life in the lies lane can be such an ordeal. Love is Non existent. The intent is to deceive. Even gain an upper hand, based on deceit. A no brainer way to go. Nothing Lovable about such an action. See

the importance of having a Love rainbow circling the body constantly. An honest retelling of an event, is the only way to go. Trust, harmony and well being are the wonderful outcomes, when truth is the ruler. Gossip and fear scaremongering only produces outcomes irrelevant to the general good. Another form of being in control."

"Another night of mind digesting and churning things over. Some of the questions, require no logical answers. There are none. When reason is fundamental to an onward progression, sometimes the conscious is unaware of the higher self and the choices made. The choices made way back whenever, are many times not understood in a present form. Again if Love is not a major intent, the learning may appear somewhat harsh. Disabilities are in the firing line very often. Interestingly enough, choices and agreements are taken on board, by the individual in the spirit of learning and experiencing. This is creation at it's best. As mentioned before, the creation world is ongoing, never stagnant. Perception can be such a hood wanker. Excuse the expression. What is seen and felt by one, is so different from the experience of another. It's like your perception of Me, is totally different from orthodox believers. Actually every one who prays to Me, do so in their own individual way. It's like that saying often used with no actuality at all.

'I know how you feel. ' They don't. There may be a slight feeling and knowing of the situation. Definitely do not understand the wholeness of what the other is going through.

That should ruffle a few thinking caps. Break time."

"An interesting phenomenon happening in your world, is the reliance on obtaining information via the many mechanical apparatuses, literally held in the hand. So much brain use is bypassed, with the reliance on artificial intelligence. And so much misinformation. A lazy use of the brain, does stump natural resources. When powerful groups utilises so called intelligent utensils for profit and control, a natural normal development goes down the drain. Healthy debates are quickly dissipated, by means of a hand held Wikipedia. Comments, whether true or false, can be rather hurtful, when applied in inappropriate ways and times."

"More on inappropriate untrue story telling. All that does, is, foster so much ill will. No winners at all."

"Presumption is another false trap, a lot of people get into. Without an actual affirmation, an incorrect assumption is taken on board, and then all sorts of things are taken out of context. Communication without facts,

is so common now. No wonder frustration is part of the norm. Hasty conclusions NOT filled and based on Love, is so hurtful and non productive.

What occurs often is inner head stewing, resulting in mean thoughts. In turn an action can have dire consequences. With so much power games around, it's essential for the governing factors to channel events their way. When control and money is involved, any means is used. Especially when fear is the main ammunition to achieve a outcome. Using the dance of fear and panic, works well for the ruthless perpetrator.

When Love, is not in the equation, and abandoned, accomplishments, are hollow and non lasting. Like building on sand. Setting up for a big collapse. And so often a dissipation takes place. When thought is on a Love track, success and joy are the sturdy foundation stones."

"How about taking a trip outside your familiar comfort zone.

Where would that be? You ask. What about another place altogether. A place where harmony and harmonics is the norm. An every day occurrence. To experience this living, all is possible by relaxing your mind and allow your thoughts to drift above your body. Just stay in this state until you feel you have stopped drifting. Once there's no feelings of movement, open your eyes and take note of what you see and feel. It's OK if you experience nothing. If that is so, reflect on your intent before starting the process."

"Good morning I thought we'd never get started.

Here's something for you. Imagination. The place of imagery. When from the place of Love, all is in order. But, and a big BUT, when fear, doubt, frustration, and hardship with hopelessness is involved, the images can be such a factor in wayward wandering. No place to go. Utter helplessness. When all these imagery forms are surrounded with Love and digested this way, an interesting outcome occurs. Again be ever vigilant, with Love being the main tool to combat these moments.

When Love surrounds thought and intent constantly, all these no hoppers don't stand a chance to do damage.

Imagination and Love together in the creative world, brings forth only joy and wonder. Rest time."

"What an interesting night. Full of chatter you were. Do you feel at ease now? I thought we'd start the day with communication and all that goes with it. Your higher self, the subconscious, is in tune with all that there is. When wording is incorrectly applied, conflict of

meaning occurs. When it's an everyday happening and the conscious is used to it, the glossing over is taken on board as the norm. Being specific in vocabulary, ensures clarity of expression. Being understood and understanding go hand in hand with a Loving relationships. Words and deeds, are the essentials in any form of communication. How applied, a result comes. Tone is another important factor. See how the setting of Love is so essential. Dark thoughts and words are like poisonous darts that can pierce and hurt. That's when a tennis match of blame can start. Your fault, my fault. Back and forth the blame game goes. Then an outcome of loveless nothingness. Something to digest."

"Something else. Bringing the future into to present. Time is such a factor in wayward wandering. Waiting for something to happen, could take for ever. Especially when it's not so good in the well being of the situation. In the meditation state, it's possible to cross all time barriers. The imagery world. Fears and doubts, are best filled with Love and then sent on their way to digest. Amazing what comes up, or goes out, after good digesting. I think we may send this chatter lot on."

"Morning greetings."

"A bit of a blank. Let's take a look at the Saturday papers and make appropriate changes in the thought mode."

"Let's chat about illness. The dealing with it. Filling the condition with Love, is the start of easing the situation. Love and medication go hand in hand. If the source of the illness is from a deep rooted inner conflict, getting in touch with the cause may alleviate the discomfort. If the reasoning is addressed, well being proceeds. When Love is ever constant in thought and deed, only Loving manifests. When constant anger, doubt and irritation is an every day happening, dis ease takes over. Love streamed the situation, results in a comforting response. Remember the Love mantle. Gather it around in such circumstances. In fact, cloak it around, at the beginning of the day and before retiring. Allow it's magic to work it's glory. Something to digest and contemplate."

"Let's chat about social media. It certainly gives scope for the unheard to be heard. The interesting thing is the intent. A lot of good intent is attributed to forces outside their control. Like it depends on Me or the universe.

Most of the goodie goodness really should originate from themselves. And then there are the comments on personality. A lot is quite derogatory. Not an ounce of Love at all. Fascinating. Behaviour, out of choice can be such a puzzlement at times. The outcomes of such goings on can come back in such a way that the wearer has no idea what hits when a consequence affects them. It's never their fault. Always the fault of the other. No responsibility whatsoever. All very well to make snide comments and get away with it. Where there is no Love in the intent, only disharmony is the ruler. Well worth thinking deeply before sending spiteful hurtful comments."

"Here's another chat subject. Competition. The importance of being first or the best. It can apply to all participants. Those doing the event or those watching. It's what is held as the primary intent. Win at any cost. This detrimental way creates ill will all around. The observer gets no satisfaction and can take it out in an unruly manner. The participant may be tempted to throw the situation into a losing result. Especially if money is involved. What you call, betting. It would be grand if there was competing to be the best in sending Love all around. Just another digestive thought."

"Another bright morning. Perhaps a rest day."

"I got caught up in a game. The names I was calling the one I didn't want to win, were pretty abominable. Really caught up in the mud slinging."

"See how easy it is to be trapped in a situation, when not fully aware and not in tune with Love action. It's always a start to be action conscious, when acknowledged."

"Morning greetings. See you had a great day yesterday exploring the wizardry world of Harry Potter. In My wizardry world, there is no conflict. My dimensions of magic are choices of Love. Never disharmony. Funny how some human stories must contain heartache and altercation, to heighten a situation. Love is an essence that permeates. Love has no adjective description. Love is. In an unconditional manner, Love never requires any form of condition. Dysfunctional behaviour is the outcome of rejection. Tone, when it be in yell or shout form, is disruptive to the Love pattern. Thoughtlessness, is cruel and hurtful to all concerned. Never in a higher realm, such actions exist. Love creates ongongly."

Our chats certainly has the mind going over and over. I'm wondering whether it's me or You. Certainly the journey is fascinating."

"Good morning I thought we'd never get started. Your receptive willingness to chat along, is an absolute delight. Continue as we are."

"The biggest threat is not constantly being enveloped in the Love mantle. This wards off falling into non Love traps. Easy to let an easy sliding into negative thoughts occur, when Love is not in the format."

"Let's recap on the how in staying within the Love surrounds. A simple set of mantras. Whenever in feelings of uncertainty. Repeat within as many times as it takes to feel at ease. All my doubts and fears I fill with Love and have them digest themselves. Another...

May the Christ Light and Power shine within me, around me, through me and from my heart. And I notice you end with a thanks to the Source. Thank you for that inclusion. These simple and effective mantras are most beneficial. And don't forget wrapping self with the Love mantle. Your questions on willfullness. Especially from youngsters. It's to do with what influences in their surrounds. In the growing intelligence, choices present themselves as what is best in achieving a satisfying outcome. If in their observations, they notice the incidents where it's easy to get away with whatever, that modelling will be taken on board. Seniors should be aware of the pitfalls of situations that impress a growing mind. Either by the behaviour or what is allowed to be viewed on entertainment devices. All these give a variety of choices on how to achieve a desired outcome. Seniors take it for granted, that what is demanded, it must be carried out. Where the modelling is erratic, the results comes up the same. Little mind's are like blotting paper. Takes on all and experiment with anything that gives the desired pleasant result. Make sure that Love is always in the surrounds of the young mind. Love essence is a radiant brightness that is infects all within It's radius. Whenever obedience is a primary condition, what is that saying, what's good for the goose is good for the gander. If the models do in a shoddy way, the young observer will do similar things. Funny how a Loving consciousness is utmost to achieve a harmonious outcome. Let's break."

"Granny duties just about over. Been an interesting year so far. Here's a topic. Punishment. Forms of punishment came about, once there was a departure from the higher self. Again choices. The saying, guilty conscious, was the instigator. I am not the perpetrator of any form of punishment. Those in the power seat created methods to ensure control over the masses. Once departure from Love occurs, fear and retribution take

hold. My guidelines are, Love yourself and others around you. Punishment is such a controller. Using fear tactics work very well in the hands of the power seeking clan. By creating opposites, those of similar aspirations, can be pulled into the deceptive game. Fear of, easily occurs when Love is out the door. It is so essential to keep Love wrapped around, constantly. How often is reward and punishment used together to achieve desired effects. The same can occur in relationships. When comparisons are used, such as, there is no Love because when a directive is not obeyed. Undue emotional blackmail."

"Hello again. Back so soon. Stay with your games and perhaps do more chatting on the plane."

"Hello hello. Seems like you've been avoiding our chat time. Are the topics getting too hot for you. Don't edit. Think about the chat later. Then you're free to edit as much as you like. ""There's been a few disasters and violent happenings around recently. What happens to those involved. Those who transit to another dimension in such an all of a sudden situation. There is much support and Love awaiting. If the thoughts at the time are of a high level, the change over is simple and orderly. It is the left behind observers who are in grief mode. Opportunity to examine how the grief mode can react.

Whether to dart hideous spiteful thoughts, or allow a release with Love to occur. In moments like these, an evolvement is in happening mode. The overall picture can be seen with a few steps back. Past belief systems and attachments compound the depth of the grief. Wild irrational acts, bring so heartache. When attachment is deep, a passing of a Loved one, can be such a traumatic time. Ease the pain by knowing, the new state of being, is a joyous reunion of self. When the Love elements are eliminated, the blame game starts and a useless fault exchange bounces around. Love does ease the unknown. Reason has no place to prolong these moments. When forwardness doesn't occur due to finding a satisfying reason, all systems stay bogged down until a Loving resolve is in order. If this is too much to take in, go play a game and allow a digestion to see what comes up. Welcome back and go."

"Here's something to digest. Better to have a knowing, rather than know. When know is in the equation, there's nowhere else to go. Being right can be so limiting. No room for discussion. Same old story, my way or no way. Knowing mode opens the door to many alternative choices. When in choice mode, it's an opportunity to really take responsibility for outcome. Once a glimpse of evolution is grasped, a deeper understanding and *response to situations becomes a Loving way of life. Have your dinner."*

"Morning greetings. Ready for another interesting thoughtful chat. How about the current fears over this virus illness. Remaining safe, requires the draping of the Love mantle around one. Not buying into the fear, with the support of the Love mantle, eliminates any chance of participating in this epidemic. Love is the overall conquering force of discomfort and dis ease. Having Loving thoughts constantly, ensures a lightness of the moment. In turn the chance of infection is minimal. Love is the powerful anti biotic. Easy to see, when Love surrounds, harmony and well being presides. OK staying in a Love lane. When tit for tat develops into revenge. Very, very dangerous. These thoughts may manifest into a serious non alignment with health. It becomes catchy when allowed to develop unchecked. Pay back time, is so so useless. All that energy on non tangible importance. Don't fall into this trap. It'll come back with such a sting. There will be no clue when it strikes. Festering thoughts have a sneaky way of manifesting. Don't be caught. Be constant with Loving thought. The magic of Love is so fixing. How's that for a morning session. Send it off and have your hand contraption handy to take up a chat when I call. Rest and play. Much Love."

"*Being cross and annoyed at self doesn't solve the problem. It only creates and manifests impatience in behaviour, which in turn can block a satisfying resolution.*"

"*It's not the cause that is at fault, it's the reaction taken on board. This reaction can bring untold damage to relationships, within or around. Imperative to wash the incident with Love, digest the situation and see what comes up. ""Agreement is a road to the Love pieces. When in this mode, harmonious harmony produces. So satisfying, so agreeable, so absolutely perfect. Commanding obedience does not give satisfaction. An inner disagreement may spoil the desired outcome. Action out of drudgery leaves grumpy outcomes. Digest and play a game.*"

"*Here we are again. Take some time out and keep your device handy in case there's something to chat about. Enjoy the day.*"

"*Sucha nothing day. Your contraption wasn't within reach when I called. So many subjects came up. And no one to take dictation. The simplicity of life is all about the Love mode. How much, how little. The measurement speak for themselves. Always when Love is involved, resolutions come Lovingly. Better go and watch your spooky show."*

"Something else to contemplate and chat about. I have mentioned Before, I create, not destroy. I have never been in the tit for tat regime.

Only those establishing a power base, thought up those ideas. Control by fear, is such a powerful weapon. Notice the same methods are in use in your everyday power seekers. Oh my, what choices and free will can do in the hands of the unscrupulous. So important not to be caught up in such goings on. Remember once in the know, Love is the safety barrier. Cloak oneself in the Love mantle and watch disagreeables evaporate. When Love is the intent, sticky situations are manageable. There is no pay back in My realm. Man created that. Uncertainty and fear are such powerful weapons. Useful for obedience. Thou shalt not, isn't My line. What is more relevant, is choose between this way and that way. Choices and taking responsibility for the action is My style. Enough for the moment. Rest up. Much Love."

"The house is filled with the energies of young folk. All in an uncomplicated world. The only agenda for them at this stage is discovery and own enjoyment."

"It is at this stage, what impresses, lingers in the memory bank. Behavioural patterns are noted carefully and each detail, married to the present understanding. If it fits, then it is applied accordingly."

"Perhaps send this chat off."

"That was a mammoth undertaking this morning. And to have all the that pieces fall into place. Leads Me on to patience. An important Love mode to have desired requests actuate. All in good time, the evolving dictates will make themselves known. Patience with a capital P, bring conclusions in a calming manner. No stress, no strain. The quiet achiever, achieves the desired outcome, with poise and joy. When in rush rush mode, so much is overlooked. Mistakes can occur (not the culprit's fault)and undue blame is dished out willy nilly. Tension can eventually bring on a not wanted violent act. Everyone looses. Just by being impatient. Fascinating how the absence of a Loving intent, can create so much chaos. Well done this morning. Your patience gave the results wanted. Enjoy the day."

"Morning greetings. Back to the normal format. What an adventure. Learnt a lot more on the workings of the mechanical world. Think you'd better go back to the small device."

"*Back so soon. Here's a chat topic. Relationship.*

The important one is with self. How self relates to self is how a relationship relates with another. Some trouble in space with the script."

"*Sometimes not a good idea to chat during your cocktail time. You may be shocked at what we chat about. Freedom of mind wandering can work when in conscious allowance. Funny enough I find I chat with you when you're in open mode. Passion of doing is an interesting chat topic. The trap is being righteously right. When in this mode, a blindness in not seeing, distorts any form of a Loving outcome. Again when Love is not in the area, dissatisfaction feelings take over. OK rest time, enjoy your wine. Different chatting in the afternoon.*"

"*Morning greetings. Feeling a bit tired are you? Keep device handy and we'll chat later.*" "*Something to always keep to the fore. Keep Love in personal surrounds constantly. If and when stress rears its ugly head, the Love threads will soothe the moment.*"

"*Here's an interesting contemplation. That movie viewed last evening will prove to be of enormous change patterns in the structure of the organization.*

Huge choices are about to be opened up. Evolvement is a happening. The Love threads are weaving It's magical magic. Watch and observe. That song.... Love is in the air. Hum it constantly and enjoy the changes."

"How about chatting about loyalty and trust. Loyalty above all, no matter what the cost can lead to big trouble. When a line is crossed, and the loyalty demands deceit and lies. That loyalty is worthlessness personified. A betrayal of self worth occurs and the trust mode is out the door.

Trust is questioned by the parties involved. Even the demanding party, deep down, questions the real reason for the loyalty. An ongoing merry go round of falsehood and uncertainty. No winners whatsoever. Love is not in the picture. Shallowness and emptiness. The result of a loyalty that falsely perpetrates lying and cheating. A loyalty that demands this type of action, goes nowhere but down the drain. A genuine loyal companion, demonstrates a trust, unshakeable and Loving. These two attributes can be such a marvellous working partnership. Must be based on Love, to fully gain those exquisite moments. Again when either is done in a blind unthinking manner, and the consequences are for greed and ill gotten goods, hard to shake the hollowness. Ease up. Chat later."

"How about chatting about loyalty and trust. Loyalty above all, no matter what the cost can lead to big trouble. When a line is crossed, and the loyalty demands deceit and lies. That loyalty is worthlessness personified. A betrayal of self worth occurs and the trust mode is out the door. Trust is questioned by the parties involved. Even the demanding party, deep down, questions the real reason for the loyalty. An ongoing merry go round of falsehood and uncertainty. No winners whatsoever. Love is not in the picture. Shallowness and emptiness. The result of a loyalty that falsely perpetrates lying and cheating. A loyalty that demands this type of action, goes nowhere but down the drain. A genuine loyal companion, demonstrates a trust, unshakeable and Loving. These two attributes can be such a marvellous working partnership. Must be based on Love, to fully gain those exquisite moments. Again when either is done in a blind unthinking manner, and the consequences are for greed and ill gotten goods, hard to shake the hollowness. Ease up. Chat later."

"Good morning. Interesting set of thoughts you had during the night. Do you mind if I butt in and make a comment."

"*Go to your device and let's chat with that. Should be interesting.*"

"*Yes your getting a handle on dealing with no no's in your life. Filling the incident with Love and then having the incident digest itself. Love does not conflict. It eases and soothes. In an illness, Love sent to the ailment will lighten and clear ways for making a different choice. When asked to digest the situation, what comes up may make a huge difference in attitude. Love in all situations is a redeeming plus. Smother doubts and fears with huge doses of the Love ingredient, clarity surfaces, and new choices are made. Simple.*

Let's tackle the other thoughts racing in and around the head. What happens when the next dimension is violently thrust upon a person. Depending on the belief, assimilation can be easy or confusing. There are many helpers and guardians to help in the transition. When victim and perpetrator are both involved, that then is very interesting. Since punishment is not a major factor in this realm, time is given to healing the cause and new effective choices are put in place. Sadness reigns among the remaining observing witnesses. Love can go out the door and spiteful revengeful feelings take over. What is not understood, can decimate thoughts of reasoning and lead to bigger bigotry to compound an already explosive situation. All action is governed by the individual belief system. The same as when and what is spoken, is via the inner beliefs. Actions precipitate the same. Revenge and violent action stems from deep hurt and rejection. Observe when the deep hurtful thoughts are not quickly addressed, and smothered with Love, outcomes are painful and non comprehended. So important to constantly keep the Love mantle wrapped around. In creation, all evolves. Violence and ill will, will dissipate eventually. Love will take it's place. No conquering done here. A natural progression evolves. Since creation was created out of Love, Love is the major factor. That should be enough for this morning. Keep your device handy, just in case I wish to disrupt your thoughts. Much Love to you, My Edward.

"Evolution takes it's time. Eventually all paths lead home to Love. Love will overcome all adversaries. Believe it and know it. Some creations take time to ward off nasty buggy bugs. Original choices got and kept them in this state for some time. Love will illuminate the way. Horrid action today will dissipate under the Love banner. So hard to be in the understanding mode when disaster and turmoil prevails. Love can have actions be seen more clearly. Clarity comes easily to those who are

doused in the Love waves. Misunderstanding is the result of a persistent following of inappropriate choices. Change the choice patterns and enjoy the prosperity of what Love has to offer. What happens in this dominion is for Me to know and for the voyeur to discover. Transition from one dimension to another is simple and orderly. All the luggage required, is a Loving set of beliefs. A few insights worth digesting. Not too confusing? And there's more to unveil. All in good time. Meanwhile stay and be aware of Love and all It's wonders. Thanks for picking up the device. Enjoy the rest of the day."

"After some more. Let's see. Let's reiterate the dealing with unwanted incidents and uneasy health issues. Send a double dose of Love to the party concerned. Have it all digest itself, and await an outcome. The higher self knows how to deal with the promoted answer. A jel will occur when the choices made are in sync. Patience and discreet sifting results in a forward motion, prompting a joyous bounce. Rest up now. Your editing mind is working overtime. Read through the scribing at a later date, and if you want to eliminate anything, feel free. Much Love."

"Too late. Channels blocked."

"The last contact, too slow to respond. Anyhow try getting your head around what was in and out of the thought Pattern during the night. Retribution. Again not in My domain. What is presented, opportunities to make a new choice. When made and activated, the slate is clear to continue in the new format. Love will and does ease past heavy inappropriate choices. The learning road takes on many avenues. Recognition is the way out of retribution. Recognising an alternative route, lightens the heavy drudgery of inappropriate behaviour. The inner self has a knowing of appropriateness. A guilty conscious is the mechanism that deals with a doing that doesn't sit well. Founders of early cults and groups, utilised this to plant fear in disobedient behaviour. Pure emotional blackmail. It's like....there is no Love, when not obedient. Love never has or ever will resort to any form of blackmail. When past actions of inappropriate behaviour weigh heavy on the mind, the time is right to lighten up with Loving choices. Smother the misbehaviour with Love, have all deeds digest themselves, and allow a new format to actual. Sounds simple. It is. Very simple. Paper day. Have a good read. See you soon. Mind you I see you all the time. Much Love."

"A good sleep in this morning. Found a new entertainment outlet. Let's start with what went through

the thought channels during the night. Reason and reasoning. This process often can delay an appropriate choice. When things don't compute, time is wasted working out a suitable answer. Interestingly enough, the higher self can point to a satisfactory conclusion. This occurs when in harmonious chords of Love. Love, in well being intent, always has perfect answers. Choosing the right reason to carry on, can be a stumbling block if pondered too long. Choice is followed through based on the personal belief at the time. When a reasoning is not appropriate and used for a personal gain, then future reasoning tries to justify the action. I find the process quite amusing. When a reason is deemed right, and it benefits the power seeking clan, some time down the line, the followers will re reason a different reason. Thus a revolt. Choices for the well being of others, with no strings attached, always has a satisfactory conclusion. A good reason to celebrate. Rest up and come back during the day."

"Health? How to be in the health mode? Daily doses of a Love bath. Have Love zap in, around, through and from the body constantly, is a sure way of staying healthy. When the vibes are in harmonious mode, the energy flow is noticeable. If appropriate food and nourishment unavailable, a Love boost can be useful. Speak some more on this later."

"Another day. Let's chat about the violence disease. Inner anger, not allowing Love to manifest. Control by absolute obedience. Mental or physical, most unacceptable. Where there is no Love involved, and obedience ignored, and uncertainty within the assailant, the personal worthlessness is taken out on a gentler subject. Happens in the bullying mode. Once Love reconnects with a subject, calmness and a clarity eventuates. See how simple how Love is and can be the pacifier in sticky situations. Violence on another only widens the violent world. Revenge and pay back, is formulated. When sparks turn into unspeakable action, the hurt and sorrow, is deep and bewildering. Love will ease pain, no matter how deep. By filling the situation with Love, a calmness and acceptance will replace the hurt and sorrow. Love is such a healing attribute. There's no winners in the violent mode. Worthlessness, self doubt are amongst the main ingredients of violent acts. Jealousy and being possessive are other forms of violence, often permitted to slip by without due concern. These can fester within and explode, with dire consequences. If these actions find their way into a daily way of living, time to bombard with a Love mantra. Love never is at war with anything. Love is the essence that eliminates any trace of war. Within It's own power, Love soothes and calms. When called upon, Love takes direction in *a knowing way to heal the crisis. All that is required, is the Loving intent. I think it's rest up time. You deserve a good session of solitaire. Enjoy."*

Another thought thinking night. Good thing you deal with the doubts and fears with a Love mantra. What about adding tradition to our chat time. Sometimes tradition can curtail progress. If the powers in office uses this form to further their foothold. It is a form of control. Keeping to the 'old' ways can delay new avenues, indefinitely. Respect and acknowledgement for well done achievements, can build a greater newness to a new development. Manners abound through self respect and self worth. How the individual wishes to be treated. Etiquette can be another form of control. Doing whatever the right way. Sensible sensitive behaviour in public, not only shows respect for the surrounds, such awareness ensures pleasantries during a get together. Just one thing leading into another. All in good time, evolution takes place. Compare it to trial and error. Choices being run through the mill, so to speak. When Love is the constant intent, a flow of ease is the outcome. There you go. Two good chat topics. Have a good day, sprucing up for your party. You'll look a million dollars. Love galore to you."

"I must say the amount of fear and doubt going on with me at the moment is a lot. Utilising Love as the healing source, I'm worried and nervous I'm not doing it right. Any suggestions?"

"A bit of a blank morning. Perhaps we could continue at a later time. Off you go."

"Let yesterday go. Always the past is the past and nothing alters it. That's why it's so important to be fully aware of intent and actuality. To alter the past, re change the present choices. No point dwelling on the outcome of past events. If the present outcomes are unsatisfactory, see if you can recall what thought thinking was going on, previous to a choice being made. If unsure, deal with the present moment, use a Love mantra and allow whatever to eventuate.

Action may not be immediate. Whatever the outcome, Love has put It's stamp on the procedure. In regards to doing it right, all is in the right lane, once Love is involved. When called upon, Love gently guides appropriate outcomes conducive to the well being of the moment. If changes are in order, so be it. Fears and doubts tackle the strengths of the belief system. They work flat out to keep situation after situation on it's toes. The important factor, be aware who's in charge. The choices seeker. When all seems impossible, now is the time to bombard with Love mantras. Repetition of a mantra greatly enhances the desired result. The impossible is made possible, always, when a Loving choice is in place. Your fears and doubts are the result of uncertainty in the thought mode. Love doesn't act out of a tit for tat regime. Love is a certainty. It only creates in the Love mode, Loveliness. Persistence is the key to attaining well being. Persistence in keeping the thought train on the positive track. Loving thought, produces satisfactory outcomes. Quite a lot of digesting to be done. Go relax and leave your doubts and fears in the Love train."

"Punishment you ponder. Not by Me. Created by those who enjoy the taste of power and control. The same group who manufactured upstairs and downstairs. Heaven and hell. Rewards for the obedient and torture for the wayward. The disobedient ones. Fear, fear works wonders for the unenlightened. And what a powerful tool. All from a knowing by use of the free will. Can you see, how at times the free will and choices lot is such a pain in the butt for Me. And to make matters' worse, supposedly My doing. Always I do out of Love. Not to destroy, pull down or punish. Rewards are not a major major in My domain. Just natural progression. An evolution that is constant. Personages confined in

small areas.....let's finish. I've lost My chain of thought. Chat later."

"I do have disappointment time when free will and choices go over the top. I and My support team are here to support all things of a well being nature. Oh yes. Where were we? Confinement. Not a sensible way to go, if improvement is a necessary requirement. Address a cause well before an error has been actioned. When situations occur that creates feelings of inadequacy, jealousies and envy can display itself. And easy ways of a procurement are sort. A big reason, no self worth. No self valuing. Unnecessary coveting for hollow trinkets. Hence a pay back system was created to maintain obedience to the system. How to deal with the bad eggs of the community, a place of isolation seemed to be a good idea. An eye for an eye policy, deemed OK by Me. Far from it. All this is starting to irritate. Must keep My cool. We'll continue later."

"Morning greetings. So much going on in the head department last night. I noticed you were tossing around definitions of Love. None really. Love is. It encompasses all to do with well being. Love has it all. Compassion, understanding, fulfilment, respect, values, peace, joy, energy, all that is beneficial and nourishing for the

individual. *Love is not a reward factory. There is no need to need, in the Love realm. The Love of, or Love to syndrome, is a factor in confusion. What can creep in, is the uncertainty of not doing, right. And when considered right, expectations of appropriate rewards. Interesting isn't it. Definition can be a stumbling block. What can happen, there is no forward movement until a reward or acknowledgement is forthcoming. Love does not demand. Love is the essence that perpetuates the knowing of appropriateness. When called upon to shine within, Love is at It's best elements. The simple mantra of invoking Love in any situation, enhances all that makes contact. Do these few ideas, give a clarity, easy to cope with. Another thing. I hear and respond to each request. It may not be the required expected answer. I will non the less, prompt new choices. When the inner belief is open, action can be satisfactory. Our chats are only that. Some thoughts to digest as an alternative. All based on Love. Love and It's attributes is such a magnificent outcome in all matters. There I think we've covered a good deal this morning. Papers day may spark some new musing. Enjoy the day. Much much Love."*

Excellent chat yesterday. Let's comment on the parade last evening. It looks like a ton of fun for the participants. Same sex Love has been quite an issue in some communities. When the interaction between two individuals of the same sex, is genuine and committed, who is hurt in such situations? Those who made the rules. The rules have been disobeyed. Such a situation is deemed asunacceptable. In some cases the punishment issued is cruel and vindictive. Genuine Love has no compromise. It is. Those of that persuasion, have been persecuted for some time and Ostracised as unclean and abnormal. Many a time, the persecutors have been afraid of similar feelings in their own lives. And to protect the status quo, insisted those of the opposite sex union is the only way to go. Funny how the fear elements play a big part in so called organised community living. When admiration and Love focus on the same sex, that is admirable in itself.

Look at some of the past sculptures in the treatment of the human frame. Many exercised in absolute beauty. It is seeing beauty in any and everything. The harm done in actual involvement of two characters is the man made commands have been ignored and disobeyed. Not acceptable. Thus the persecution. Does it break down family values? Why ask such a thing? Family values are as strong as the foundations founded on. When Love reigns supreme in such a household, happenings are taken in their stride. Understanding and compassion opens the door to a more tolerant society. Relationships of any form, require these elements for a harmonious union. Some pondering to digest. Love is always the key ingredient. Rest up. Catch up later."

"Another comment. Watching with you, last night's parade, looks like a lot of fun. Freedom of expression can be such a release. It's a good term, gay. Everyone is so happy in like minded individuals. Wanted to make a comment. Thanks for transcribing."

"Another happening in your world. The fear of contacting an illness, creating much concern. Avoidance with fear, only draws more attention to the situation. Smother the fear with Love and relax into that mode. Attention to, and too much dwelling on the virus, can unnecessarily draw the condition into an actuality. The Love mantle and mantra, very helpful in this situation. Stay focused. Thanks for the Chat.

Morning greetings. A little surprise get together last night for you. Very nice and a specialness about it. These touches in life are so rewarding. And you didn't overdo it. Good to have a good night's sleep, with feelings of well being. It is such a good idea to stay wrapped in the Love mantle. Looks like your head is still fuzzy from the drinks of last night. We can catch up later in the day."

"Oh the next day already. Your TV certainly had you thinking last night. Speaking on gender, I AM who I AM. I am not a long bearded wise looking Santa Claus. It's interesting how the belief system stays in a certain frame of mind. And maintains a picture to enable a form of communication. I listen, prompt and suggest another choice. Creations are ongoing. Re inventing, reforming, expanding, challenging. The cycle is one of astonishment, wonder and completion. When the flow, flows in harmony with the universe, Love is the ultimate conclusion. Still somewhat weary. Come back later. Meanwhile stay in the Love mode. Much Love."

"A bit of a blank morning. Perhaps we could continue at a later time.

Off you go."

"Let yesterday go. Always the past is the past and nothing alters it. That's why it's so important to be fully aware of intent and actuality. To alter the past, re change the present choices. No point dwelling on the outcome of past events. If the present outcomes are unsatisfactory, see if you can recall what thought thinking was going on, previous to a choice being made. If unsure, deal with the present moment, use a Love mantra and allow whatever to evenuate. Action may not be immediate. Whatever

the outcome, Love has put It's stamp on the procedure. In regards to doing it right, all is in the right lane, once Love is involved. When called upon, Love gently guides appropriate outcomes conducive to the well being of the moment. If changes are in order, so be it. Fears and doubts tackle the strengths of the belief system. They work flat out to keep situation after situation on it's toes. The important factor, be aware who's in charge. The choices seeker. When all seems impossible, now is the time to bombard with Love mantras. Repetition of a mantra greatly enhances the desired result. The impossible is made possible, always, when a Loving choice is in place.

Your fears and doubts are the result of uncertainty in the thought mode. Love doesn't act out of a tit for tat regime. Love is a certainty. It only creates in the Love mode, Loveliness. Persistence is the key to attaining well being. Persistence in keeping the thought train on the positive track. Loving though, produces satisfactory outcomes. Quite a lot of digesting to be done. Go relax and leave your doubts and fears in the Love train."

Punishment you ponder. Not by Me. Created by those who enjoy the taste of power and control. The same group who manufactured upstairs and downstairs. Heaven and hell. Rewards for the obedient and torture for the wayward. The disobedient ones. Fear, fear works wonders for the unenlightened. And what a powerful tool. All from a knowing by use of the free will. Can you see, how at times the free will and choices lot is such a pain in the butt for Me. And to make matters worse, supposedly My doing. Always I do out of Love. Not to destroy, pull down or punish. Rewards are not a major major in My domain. Just natural progression. An evolution that is constant. Personages confined in small areas.....let's finish. I've lost My chain of thought. Chat later."

"I do have disappointment time when free will and choices go over the top. I and My support team are here to support all things of a well being nature. Oh yes. Where were we? Confinement. Not a sensible way to go, if improvement is a necessary requirement. Address a cause well before an error has been actioned. When situations occur that creates feelings of inadequacy, jealousies and envy can display itself. And easy ways of a procurement are sort. A big reason, no self worth. No self valuing. Unnecessary coveting for hollow trinkets. Hence a pay back system was created to maintain obedience to the system. How to deal with the bad eggs of the community, a place of isolation seemed to be a good idea. An eye for an eye policy, deemed OK by Me. Far from it. All this is starting to irritate. Must keep My cool. We'll continue later."

"Morning greetings. So much going on in the head department last night. I noticed you were tossing around definitions of Love. None really. Love is. It encompasses all to do with well being. Love has it all. Compassion, understanding, fulfilment, respect, values, peace, joy, energy, all that is beneficial and nourishing for the individual. Love is not a reward factory. There is no need to need, in the Love realm. The Love of, or Love to syndrome, is a factor in confusion. What can creep in, is the uncertainty of not doing, right. And when considered right, expectations of appropriate rewards. Interesting isn't it. Definition can be a stumbling block. What can happen, there is no forward movement until a reward or acknowledgement is forthcoming. Love does not demand. Love is the essence that perpetuates the knowing of appropriateness. When called upon to shine within, Love is at It's best elements. The simple mantra of invoking Love in any situation, enhances all that makes contact. Do these few ideas, give a clarity, easy to cope with.

Another thing. I hear and respond to each request. It may not be the required expected answer. I will non the less, prompt new choices. When the inner belief is open, action can be satisfactory. Our chats are only that. Some thoughts to digest as an alternative. All based on Love.

Love and It's attributes is such a magnificent outcome in all matters. There I think we've covered a good deal this morning. Papers day may spark some new musing. Enjoy the day. Much much Love."

Another comment. Watching with you, last night's parade, looks like a lot of fun. Freedom of expression can be such a release. It's a good term, gay. Everyone is so happy in like minded individuals. Wanted to make a comment. Thanks for transcribing."

"Another happening in your world. The fear of contacting an illness, creating much concern. Avoidance with fear, only draws more attention to the situation. Smother the fear with Love and relax into that mode. Attention to, and too much dwelling on the virus, can unnecessarily draw the condition into an actuality. The Love mantle and mantra, very helpful in this situation. Stay focused. Thanks for the Chat."

"Morning greetings. A little surprise get together last night for you. Very nice and a specialness about it. These touches in life are so rewarding. And you didn't overdo it. Good to have a good night's sleep, with feelings of well being. It is such a good idea to stay wrapped in the Love mantle. Looks like your head is

still fuzzy from the drinks of last night. We can catch up later in the day."

"Oh the next day already. Your TV certainly had you thinking last night. Speaking on gender, I AM who I am. I am not a long bearded wise looking Santa Claus. It's interesting how the belief system stays in a certain frame of mind. And maintains a picture to enable a form of communication. I listen, prompt and suggest another choice. Creations are ongoing. Re inventing, reforming, expanding, challenging. The cycle is one of astonishment, wonder and completion. When the flow, flows in harmony with the universe, Love is the ultimate conclusion. Still somewhat weary. Come back later. Meanwhile stay in the Love mode. Much Love."

"Ah ha a mid morning chat. Very impressive. Looks like your birthday celebrations are coming together nicely. Just let the events meld into each other. And without stress or strain, enjoy the flow. Your milestone is worth the celebrations. In the years to this stage, you've tuned to possibilities on offer. Readjusted choices and here we are. You and Me like two loving chums chatting obstacles aside.

So a little voyaging this morning. Getting into a relaxing mode.

Hear from you soon."

"Morning greetings. Your car trip was easy and enjoyable. Wonderful how the countryside has rejuvenated after all those cleansing fires. Nature has that knack of bouncing back. In either a fresher look or completely new. Evolution in motion. Dealing with your present dilemmas has you on your toes. Feeling hard done by, and reversing thoughts of ill will, Love thoughts are the quickest method in rectifying the situation. When there is a constant flow of poor me thoughts, Love thoughts in reversal mode, can ease the bewildering reasoning. When you feel you are unfairly wronged, then examine what is the main elements that bring this feeling. Allow a Loving dart to pierce the wronged thought and let them digest themselves. Filling thoughts of this nature, with Love, will bring harmony and a balance to the situation. Oh I see you struggling that remedy. Let the situation digest itself and see what happens. Now go and have an enjoyable day. Nice to be chatting in your Sydney surrounds. Chat later."

"Another thing. Being hard done by, and misunderstand, is an opportunity in engulfing Love to the situation. Different thought waves may interrupt constantly, however persistent rethinking about choices,

with Love, clarity will surface and what seemed unfair, will dissipate into the not so hard basket."

"Let's look at time. So much revolves as it evolves. Divided into it's component sections, past, present and future, very interesting which is the most important. With Love as the main element in each, each part will be a fulfilling experience. Love intent that govern the actuality, all is possible to have a smooth joyous journey. Time can be restrictive when Loving thought is restricted. See how so much revolves and evolves Love. The one daily ingredient that can jettison chores in the delightful realm. Future space can be such a continuing of the present that is grounded in Love. Allowing the future to develop an already learnt experience, brings an abundance of exquisite joy. Go digest and have a good day."

"The present is the powerful moment. Utilise it."

"Loyalty and honour constantly is a subject that can be pondered.

These attributes are effective when self is loyal to, and honours self. Impossible to practice what is not a substantial way of life. Blind loyalty and praise for personal gain, and no real conviction of any integrity, leads to a mass hysteria of useless wasteful outcomes. Each and all have a thinking device to sort out the appropriate and unacceptable.

When Love is not a major factor in thought decision, and personal gain, no matter what the cost, is the desired outcome, all manner of disruptive happenings occur. Without Love in the main mix, hollowness is the unfulfilled experience. A self loyal to self, perfectly honours self. Such an easy format. In your world where technology is advancing so rapidly, it's easy to let the new hood wink into falsehood. The creation of easy quick methods, doesn't necessarily get one out of an unpleasant situation. Modern technology is there to serve and open doors for further creations. When technology and newness is compassionate and into well being, amazing harmonious societies come forth. Making every day living easier is such an honourable purpose. Love is loyal to such ideas. See how the two intertwine into stable productive acceptable harmonious living conditions, when doused with Love.

Noticed your Mass attendance, had the story of Transfiguration.

What is important is that as Evolvement in the personality occurs, such manifestations take place in a

Love filled soul. So much is available for anyone who abides in the Love stream. Worth time to contemplate and digest. Celebration time two days away. Enjoy it slowly and with an inner enjoyment. Don't overdo the stimulants. Go enjoy the day."

"When there is a connection with the higher self, Love opens the Transfiguration door. The soul shows and shines in all its glory. Available to each and all. It's that little sparkling essence in all of creation that access this wonderment. Bye."

"Good Morning and best wishes on your anniversary day. Tomorrow a birthday celebration. Such a festive time. Education and relevant information is on your mind this morning. Education is the evolving wonders of information. As the occupants of the planet evolved in knowing, creation expanded. To educate, is a Loving task that allows potential to shine. When educated in greed and self serving ideals, disruptive happenings occur. Where Love is shut out, the unconscious will rebel. The inner self only knows the appropriate way. Eventually a tiredness of inappropriate doing manifests. The unconscious is highly educated and doesn't take well to false information. Choices give a pathway of clarity or hidden agenda. When the educators present and pass on

information that enhance, Love of widening knowledge, occurs. Information is not for the few. Elite education is not for the few. Education broadens communication channels and the chance of harmony and agreeable co-existence. All this happens with Love is the intent. See the simplicity in ensuring Love begins all, endorses all, and actions all. Love is never far from actuality. To be fully attuned and educated in the Love manner, brings joy to all Endeavours. False information, purposely distributed to ensure control over the uneducated and keep them in the dark, so to speak, is an absolute no no in My book. Once injustice is twigged, revolution and angry action can take place. The higher realm will always eventually make itself known.

Mass control for the purpose of individual acquisition, often results in the controlled, desiring the same. And acquiring it can cause much pain and upheaval. The uneducated only know one road. That is up. The discrepancies demand a filling. The natural way of evolving.

That should be sufficient fodder for contemplation. Enjoy your anniversary day. Much Love."

Birthday greetings and good morning. You are about to start another decade. Within the last eighty years, Love calls have been heeded and here we are chatting away like old chums of yore. Love these moments so much. Life is what choices are made. Conscious Loving thought is always the key ingredient to successful outcomes. Let's chat about altered state. Switching from one dimension to another. Can be a big ask task for some. Depends on the depth of attachment to temporal articles. Such times divide a normality to accountability. Love measuring procedure. How full is the container. All the way, half way, just a drop. There is always at least 380mls of Love in each and all. Whether accessed and built on, is up to the individual. Stop for now and take your good wishes."

"That was some celebration last night. A room full of Love, all in your direction. Wonderful how intent can preclude the actuality and outcome is so satisfying. Perhaps a day of rest up time."

A gentle recovery day yesterday. Such a wonderful celebration the night before. Let's chat about opportunity. Catching inner calls to do. Intuition. When in Love mode, easy to activate the impulse. These promptings are from the higher self region. They can enhance and direct to a satisfactory outcome. These opportunities are there, constantly. Grabbing by the horns, so to speak. Not being in tune with a Love mantra. Inner listening is filled with inconsequential chatter. Doesn't hear or heed helpful promptings. Opportunities pushed aside. Without Love in the main mix, erroneous pursuits are the order of the day. Greed and lack of compassion results in turmoil and utter failure of purpose. Let's rest up. Much Love to you."

"What a period of fear and panic happening all around at present. Glad to see you are wrapping up in the Love mantle. With Love in the equation, helplessness evaporates. When an epidemic occurs, a chance to take stock of personal choices. Things slow down. After the initial mad rush to instigate a safety net, the road to normality unfolds via the Love path. When Love flows within, around, through and from the personality, clarity will surface. Panic becomes an opportunity to really take fear by the horns and realign choices. Love will play It's part and have an ordered solution return. Love is the essence that perpetuates joy, energy and purpose. Out of chaotic situations, Love is the absolute soothing remedy. Always be aware of the Love remedy. Within, around, through and from you, Love is there to guide through any turmoil. I see one more day of birthday celebrations before heading homeward. Relax and enjoy. The choices you've made are returning you, fulfilling, memorable joyous memories. Well earned. Well done. Keep up with the chatting whenever. Much Love to you."

"Hello and good morning. Looks like the virus epidemic is creating plenty of fear still. As in any situation like this, remaining fixed and focused on the Love mantra, fear and doubt is calmed. Love is the essence that open resources able to off set the panic situation. Remember to allow Love to flow within, around, through and from in every conscious moment. The calling of Love, comfort's distressing thought and uneasy guide lines. Clothe self with a Love cloak and mantle, and experience a calmness and safety able to resonate with others. Lead by example. Much Love to you."

"Chat when you can. Safe travels."

Welcome home. Such a wonderful time you had to celebrate this milestone of your life. 80years on the planet. And you and I chatting away about My favourite subject. Love. Looks like the virus epidemic is the present day highlighter. You do well, by remaining in and close to the Love pieces and mantra. It is Love that calms the panic and overrides the situation. Love will address the uneasiness and heal whatever requires to be healed. All what is required, intent, with Love being the main ingredients. Even if doubt and fear is making itself felt. Love can override and will do so, when called upon.

Being in a safety zone, Love is the essence that suits the occasion at all times. All done with ease. This epidemic can dissipate once Love is involved and called upon. When solutions are in front of the nose, so to speak, they can be overlooked as an impossibility. Reasoning can get in the way, especially when not in the scientific proven norm. Funny how acceptable norm, can shut out a natural process that requires a simplistic approach. Love essence and workability is there always, with the Love intent. Can't stress this enough. When in doubt, cover in Love. That's all for now. Much good will and Love."

Well hello. Having a blank moment. I've been wanting to chat, but you've been avoiding our chat time. Doubt and fear is raging all around. Remember keep abreast with the Love mantra and action It's rays at the slightest feeling of uncertainty. When you give in to these things, what happens, is a slow down or even a stop, of any progressive action. Fear and doubt are stumbling blocks that hinder you. Illness and being in a dis ease mode, is made manageable when Love is in the equation. The use of modern medicine and a Love innovation can work the miracle. All achieved with ease. The more fear is fed, the more the outcome will be an unwanted visitor. Love with all It's benefits overcomes any panic scenario. Stay aware of the benefits and enjoy the prosperity of whatLove brings. Thanks for the catchup. Enjoy your day."

"Given yourself quite a break from the chat room. Don't put pressure on yourself, with having to do all the time. At the moment, there is so much going on. Fear and panic appears to be the order of the day. When you hesitate in Loving thought, and buy into the pandemonium, confusion and doubt rears its troublesome head. Remember Love is the elements of calm and clarity. Love only knows one way to go. And that is for well being. When invoked, Love does what Love does. It knows no other way, but calm and clarity. Trust Me, Love is the guide for a fulfilment in the ongoing search of a lighter way of living. When bombarded with doubt and irritation at what is currently happening, draw back and have Love flow the question mark. Feeling better and in harmony? Rest up and let's chat whenever. Enjoy your day and you."

"Thank you. Feel grounded already."

"Well well. A mid morning chat. What did you want to hear. Staying on top of things. How about staying in the present. On top of things is only a temporary feeling

of achievement. It lasts as long a good burp. When the feeling is one of conquering a situation, be prepared to be surprised with the wind taken out of the sails. To conquer intimates a war going on. A war with any issue, concludes with an empty sense of accomplishment. Warring or at conflict with, opposes all Love input. When these elements are forcefully active, the unconscious shakes It's head in complete disagreement. Then a tug of war of choices take place. Even in times of indecision, choices play an important role. Then a forward move can occur, once responsibility is sorted out. Responsibility is what Love, loves. Perhaps time to break and do every day chores. Add this to the manuscript writings."

Welcome back. Noticed you've been in the land of doubt and fear for the last few days. Remember to invoke a Love mantra at such times. Love is the essence that eliminates the outcome of doubt and fear. Love has no opposite. It's function is one of satisfactory outcomes. When invoked It only knows one way to go, and that is for betterment. Love works hand in hand with evolution. Evolution is education in motion. Thought evolves as education expands. So much time is spent on reasoning circumstances out. Going forward can be hindered trying to sort things out. Let's look at leadership again. Real leadership is when in collective mode, where

Love is the intent and put in place. Leaders who bully and lie to gain power, are the real stumbling block in a harmonious community. Eventually a thinking group will question the intent of the leader and group. When things go against Love, the inner self will search for a resolution. Love cannot and will not be hood winked. Love only knows a fulfilment that is one of joy and happiness.

Imagine if you will, a world of utter contentment. Servitude chores done by robots. Man spends time in the creative fields. Competition is for the unenlightened. Those who choose to be constantly in a better mode than others, insist on proving self worth by playing defeatist games.

Collective leadership, with Love being the main ingredients, is an idealway to bring and give stability in any community. When personal gain and greed is in the equation, again a thinking group will question such actions. Then depending on the depth of discontent, a revolt and bloodshed, can take place. Unsatisfactory for all concerned. In this time of virus scaring and uncertainty, Love is the essence that perpetuates safety and certainty of overcoming the situation. Having Love cover the world of the epidemic, results in a return to a satisfactory conclusion. Let's leave it there. Go play a game and allow digestion to take place."

"Welcome back. Having quite a few doubts going on in your head. Don't fret. Remember to place such times in the Love mode.

Good Morning. Long time no chat. Confusion is rife for you at the moment. Remember your association with the Love mode. Call on the mantle to swamp you with It's essence and being."

"The present day crisis is an opportunity to remake health choices. Entering into different agreements about well being and sourcing appropriate support lines. Love mantras are the ideal resoluters. When called upon in genuine heartfelt requests, Love will respond with the protective armour required. Despair and hopelessness are taken under It's wing and are replaced with Love attributes. This takes place once responsibility is taken on board. Even if it is not apparent there is no fault for the considered disaster. In no way would I start such a mess, for what ever reason. I don't do that sort of thing. Powerful narrow minded individual groups utilises fear from the unseen, as a means of utter control. Education and Evolvement is the process that questions. I create

out of Love. I have never created to punish or destroy. Free will is the instigator. Conveniently used in making a power base. From My point of view, at times highly amusing. Not funny for those caught up in the game. Fear of unseen and nasty looking creatures, has no place in My domain. I have the knowingthat eventually all will return to the original source. And that is Love and It's domain."

"The idea of Me being some sort of pay back monster is of nonsense to the fullest. Just think, what sort of creator, creates to pull down. Definitely not Me. Power hunger individuals gave the ignorant punishment if not obeyed."

"Morning greetings. Quite a lot of musing going through that head of yours. Let Me reiterate. When prayed to, I certainly listen. I, together with My helpers, will suggest different choices and point to appropriate resolutions. If the petitioner is seeking well being, the inner self will hear and respond accordingly. I never leave a Loving request unanswered. I think we have chatted enough to make conversations with others, more than interesting. Transfer this to the manuscript writings. Much Love."

"You've lost Me for a moment or two. Just think of the epidemic and It's consequences. The fear, the doubt.

My dear chatter it's time to discuss a resolution. Love and It's marvels is a road to recovery. Love only knows one way to go. And that is for well being. Utilise It's power now. Take courage and take time to inform others on what you know. When others express the desire to have Love rule, be rest assured so much fall into place.

Oh My dear Edward you and Me chatting is such a delight.

Compassion is such a virtue.

Not does it open to amazing blessings, it manifests tranquillity in the immediate surrounds. Being in a listening mode and allowing a compassionate response allows the Love magic weave enormous benefits.

Rewards abound in a million fold when action is governed by Love and It's attributes. The rewards is a by product of such actions. All is nullified when intent is for a reward. Spontaneity is the order of the day.

All the fears and doubts tackling your thought system, is part of the process in having Love be a strong component in dealing with this virus outbreak. Again by just invoking Love, allow Love to flow within, around, through and from the pandemic. That is all. Love knows how to deal with the situation. The outcome will always be in the well being of the the recipient. Now go and digest this and stay calm and collected. Blessings and much Love to you."

"Another day, another round of dealing with doubts and fears. With so much going on around you, your faith in the Love mode is being tested fully. Remember allow Love to do and deal with the situation. All it takes is a Love intent calling. Love will assess the situation and action It's rays of well being. Trust in the Love mantle is all that is required. Sounds too easy. It is. Love only knows one way to go. And that is for well being. Relax and let Love do It's knowing. Once the pandemic passes, and a normality takes place, be prepared for the many changes about to surprise. Some lessons may have been learnt, and a lot of old thinking discarded. A Loving outlook, will be in perfect order to have life be easier and fulfilling. Looks rosy, doesn't it. More thoughtfulness will be the order of the day. Love will continue to stream It's essence. Let's stop for a moment. I see your thought system is going into overdrive. Enjoy the possibility."

Come back when you are ready for a chat. Meanwhile enjoy the day."

"Again another night of mind digesting. The longer you ponder, the more confusing things appear. When *in figuring mode, and nothing adds up, best to allow Love to flow within the questioning. Once this is in motion, a clarity will replace the confusion. Examining the life and purpose of Jeshua Ben Joseph, takes an inner contemplation that can produce further reasoning of bewilderment. The main lesson at this time of the year, is that the death process, doesn't finish on this planet. In dying, it is the movement of one dimension to another. When Love has been the main ingredients of the life, the transition is one of ease and joy. The Good Friday story is gruesome and riddled with forgiveness of sin. The sin of that version is the in-firing of personal guilt, on human frailties.*

All postulated by control personalities for their own power fuelled needs. The underlying virtue of the story, is about conquering the stigma of death. And He did. His amazing attributes enabled Him to journey the journey without any form of pain, whatsoever. That's worth digesting. Enjoy this day and the whole of the Easter mysteries. Much Love for your persistence."

"Interesting times at the moment. What with today's religious beliefs, coping with a lot of it, is hard going for you. You are questioning the impact of sin and It's consequences. Sin is a manufactured power tool to have followers be subjective to those who control. Sin is

something that goes against the norm of decency. Taking advantage of this, the word sin was incorporated into the hall of unworthiness. Sin was made to be an affront to the Creator and punishable by dire means. Namely, HELL. Fire being a painful experience, was the a logical scare and fearsome example. Jeshua Ben Joseph showed that death is but a transition from one dimension to another. Nothing to do with taking on the wrong doings of man, and seeking appeasement from the Creator, Me. As I've mentioned, free will is the instigator for choice. Man is responsible for the actions under this umbrella. For Me to demand retribution for wrong doings, doesn't compute with Me. My world is one of Love. And Love doesn't have a revengeful note in It's psyche. Something to digest and be aware of your choices.

Now break and get your Saturday reading. Thoughts to walk by. Enjoy."

"The subject of Forgiveness. In My eyes, I am not offended when rules made by man are broken. Choices are made by the offender, and forgiveness come the offended. Compassion is the instigator of Forgiveness. When a person feels slighted or wronged, then is the opportunity to forgive. Love via forgiveness, is an absolute ideal opportunity to shine in the moment. Forgiveness stabilises harmony and brings about a

true Loving connection between the parties concerned. Especially a good time to contemplate such an action, during this Easter period. A time when so much has been overcome. Especially the fear of death. Created creations evolve. Such a learning abundance of exquisite joy. Once choices fall into line with the inner source, heavens of wonderment open, so to speak. Stay in harmony with compassion and flourish in the Love outcome. Perhaps transfer the chat to the manuscript writings. Enjoy the Easter period."

"Morals. They are the inner beliefs of the individual. They give guidelines. They are not what is ordained by those who command obedience. Morals are Me given hints at doing the appropriate action. Education and the Evolvement process, point the way. Thanks for breaking cocktail hour to have a chat."

"Not so receptive this morning. We can come back later."

"Still in the land of doubt. I thought the idea of Me and you chatting, you would unhesitatingly transcript, no editing. I know a lot of the ideas put forward are questionable and entirely new to digest. By staying with Me, an opportunity to explore new and different

perceptions. Rewards and punishments. Achievements is rewards in My domain. Punishment is a self inflicted process. Punishment attributed to Me, was to make the power stand more effective. Definitely not Me. My world is based on Love. And Love and punishments are not bed mates. Justice is another interesting topic. It is not a criterion in My domain, as it is an ongoing process. When all action is motivated by Love, there is no call for justice. Revenge and pay back is another outcome of free will. Choices. When a situation is lacking Love in It's intent, a belief is enacted. Especially one instilled by a power base that demands obedience to it's rules. Some of the rules are accorded to Me. Not so. Far from the truth. Truth such a bandied around word and deed. As I've mentioned so many times, My creations are all out of Love. And Love never works alongside revenge or punishment. Those things are the instruments of control hunger individuals, determined to be obeyed, no matter the cost. Fear instigators who know how to appeal to the uneducated. Go and play a game now. Come back soon."

"Let's do Obedience again. This little do as you're told, takes place in many forms during the day. Public opinion is swayed one way or the other when in judgement of other's action. When the judged don't

abide, condemnation, fly sparks everywhere. Obedience by one's call, rules an unhappiness that falls in the control domain."

"Timing. A good subject. When is the right time? The present is the actuality of time. What happens now, is the real thing. Good timing gives a boost to choices. A feeling of everything is on side. The feeling of missing out because of supposedly bad timing is another opportunity to revise choices, rethink, re choose, and take responsibility. Acknowledging choices, rather than blaming the situation, has Love administer It's talents. Love does not have power of any form in It's equation. Love does the request and the rest is up to the seeker.

Thanks for the afternoon chat."

"You've finished voyeurising the game world for a while.

Lovely to continue our chatting. Let's continue on Love when called upon. Love actuates when called upon by the individual. When an individual calls to Love for support, Love responds as Love knows how. Love's intent is only for well being. This process cannot be transferred from one to another. The Love process occurs only when called upon by the individual. Love respects individual choices. May not agree, and when a new choice is made, Love is there with flying colours. So rewarding when Love is called within, around, through and from the personality. I seem to harp so much on this. At the moment, your planet and place of residence is experiencing an amazing fall in manufactured pollution, due to shut down laws in place. It's a time for Mother earth to replenish It's self. Interesting to observe changes, if any, once the pandemic passes. Now is the time for each and all to call Love into each life. Imagine the combination of each and all in the Love mantle. The respect and responsibility being shared will bring such harmonious harmony into being. I get quite excited at just the thought. All possible, with Love in the equation. Might be an idea to transfer to the main manuscript. Much Love to you. Be kind to yourself and enjoy the abundant rays of Love.

You are remembering war casualties today. Such a futile exercise. By now evolution has reunited many souls to their original source. Choices of doing again would be in place. The more the experience is painful, the more the learning. Wanton taking of life, is such a stigma on evolution. When Love is left out, and power and control is the one aim, confusion and anguish is the unfortunate outcome. When the oppressed combines their

Love mantle, the oppressor lose their original purpose. The funny thing is that both warring sides claim I am with their side. I'm an observer in these conflicts. After many years of utter bullying, the Love mantle threads It's way into a different way of doing.

You are not flowing with Me at the moment. Stop, rest up."

"A thought. In this pandemic time, surrender to Love. By doing so, and allowing Love space to weave It's attributes, Love enfolds the virus in It's mantle. The virus readjusted it's self and safety is assured. The calling of Love, is simplicity in itself. Just a probe during relaxation time. Digest."

"A dying time is such a difficult time for the observers. When transference from one dimension to another, the mortal side is effected. During an pandemic many may fall in line with the expectation. Without the invocation of Love, understanding and acceptance is a tall order. Requesting Love into the equation, resolves a painful happening.

Funny you're interrupting cocktail hour. Belief is a fundamental action of choice. When belief is the operating factor, sometimes time to re assess choices.

When a belief is enacted, sometimes dissatisfaction can be the outcome. Soul and Love are always in harmonious outcome. When a belief tries to overthrow, the internal conflict is interesting to observe. Nothing happens. Love is left out the door and turmoil, within the experiencing bring doubt and fear. Let's chat again tomorrow. Much Love."

"Capable ignorance, burying ones head in the sand, is no excuse for non reaction. Particularly when and where violence is occurring. A virus cannot deal with the properties of Love. Love is not into power Or a one upmanship. It is an actuality that can and does ease the situation. Thanks for breaking your cocktail time. Come and chat in the morning. In your News selection, empathetic in on cost. In My world is it what is learnt. Go and eat and try to connect tomorrow morning. Much Love."

"The amount of life ending by one's own hand, is getting larger as a depressing set of circumstances occur. Where there is no Love in the equation what appears as an easy way out, hopelessness presents in the form of a suicide. This may appear to solve the problem by taking a short cut to the other dimension. It doesn't. In the evolution of everything, another round of living is back *on the cards. Respect and responsibility are ingredients for forward progressive happenings in a life's journey. Ending the life prematurely entails another chance to reconsider choices. Once the Love bonds are taken on board, clarity shines newness of attitude. Choices are definite, and done with ease. Perhaps time to forward the current chats. Your enthusiasm is wanning somewhat. Just letting the flow happen, will be easier on your doubts and fears. Is it time to have a longer break? There are so many distractions in our chatting. Transfer the present writings to the main manuscript.*

Meanwhile have all your doubts and fears be in the Love mode.

Much Love."

"Welcome back. You've been playing with your friends on the internet. That's ok. Choices are yours to make. Some of the choices by others are causing much concern at the moment. What is done by others, is what they do. You can counteract by surrounding self with the Love mantle and send the Love back to the source of the concern. If harm is meant, with your Love shield in place, those agro intents return to the sender. In many cases, it can inflame the instigator, especially if out of tune with Love. Nice to have you back. Now go and surround yourself with the Love mantle. And stay in that mode."

"*Good morning I thought we'd stay with choices. Taking responsibility for each choice and the outcome, points in which direction the incident will go. When Love is left out, the result is often hurt, misunderstanding, and emotional reaction that leads to bitterness and unnecessary discord. Choices involved in deceit and greedy gain, leave a lasting reaction that leads to bitterness and revenge. There is no win in this situation. Just heartache, dissatisfaction, emptiness. For the perpetrator, hollowness.*

Life revolves around choices. Outcomes are either Love and fulfilling, or…"

"*That's where we stopped yesterday. You were having trouble in allowing a flow to take place. Shall I complete that last sentence. Outcomes are either Love and fulfilling or a straying collection of confusion. Not much fulfilment in the latter. Love is a complete ongoing higher values action. It has no agenda but to enlighten, direct and bring to the original created creation. When on a road of Love intent, hurdles are swept aside. Ease in all doings is the normal. When choices are acknowledged, opportunity time to re-choose choices. Keep and move on, or splash about in pools of uncertainty. The latter, leaves the self, empty and unfulfilled. Without Love, gain meanders in limbo.*

Especially when gain is gained by deceit, lies and fear scaremongering. So important to be forever on guard against the world of deceptive gain. The instigator thinks, the power control is in place indefinitely. No, no, no. Suppression eventually is overturned by the higher self of the undertroden. Quite a lot to think about. Stay in the Love mode and have Love deal with the doubts and fears. Remember when called upon, Love does the request without hesitation. Always for the well being of the individual.

Enjoy your day. Much Love."

"Nice to have you back on track. Dealing with personal disappointment or being slighted and unfairly wronged. Happenings that can be an every day hazard. Most depends on what is taken on board by the individual. When an anger develops and allowed to fester unchecked, the internal damage can be disastrous. Best way to cope. Surround self with the Love mantle and send a Love message back to the source. When there is a feeling of being unfairly bombarded with undesirable untruths, now is the time to reply with strong Love energies. Allow Love to handle the finer details. Put the

moments in the doubts and fears basket, fill with Love, and have them digest themselves."

"Even now you're dealing with an issue that is causing undue concern and negative thoughts. You are trying to make sense of the situation and applying much Love to culprit. By just invoking Love into the equation, all you have to do, is, step back and allow Love to weave It's attributes. Easier said than done, you are thinking. Persistence is the operative word. In time, an unfolding occurs. When that happens, time to review choices. And all sequences will fall into place. Rest now. Gather the Love mantle, wrap It around and walk in safety. Much Love your way."

"So much going on in that head of yours. Your choice of TV shows add to the confusion. War and anything to do with war is not in My domain. When I am called upon to do battle, the request is a disillusioned one. All I do is observe, note the wasteful loss of life. The futility of the event and AM grateful for the amount of support given to the new comers into the next dimension. The Loving work of the various beings in the new dimension, be they angels, orbs or guides, is immeasurable. A real busy time. Each individual treated with their own unique measure of support and guidance.

Break now. Don't take such a long time to chat."

"That was quick. Thanks for picking up thoughts so quickly.

When praise is sent My way, for Warring efforts, just another use of unseen power, to keep the power game going."

"It may be time to consider putting our chats in journal form. You seem to be somewhat slower in allowing a flow to take place. Understandable. So many new ideas to digest. Let's see if an opportunity arises. Much Love to you."

It was about this time the messaging was getting too much to transcribe. I kept editing so much that the flow was becoming more static. Keeping a handle of the chat was in a rebellion mood. At times I would blank out the flow. So many distractions happening in the world. To me Love was a solution and getting a strong message out there seemed such an impossible task.

"If you want to cease chatting, it's Al-right with Me. Remember you started our association with your answering My call. Something else to contemplate. Revenge and pay back. Absolutely a no win situation.

When I am called upon to give a hand, that is entirely out of the rules. That is not My domain, it's the domain of free will and choices. I watch over and observe all of creation. Outcomes are the way of choices. Thanks for picking up.

Why so much on Love you ask? Love is that gift of Mine that is an integral part of My creations. The choice is the individual's if that is requested. Love is immeasurable. Has no agenda. It is a guiding light in confused situations. When called upon, Love reconciles. It does not war or battle with anyone or anything. Love is a constant connection with Me. It is the afterthought I installed to deal with the free will and choice situations. When called upon in hopeless situations, Love will clarify. I cannot stress enough the wonders of It's actions. When called on to just do the appropriate resolution, without any specific outcome, Love will fill the gaps for the well being of the request. Love has an insight that is exquisitely only what Love will do. I see your head is turning a hundred miles an hour. Rest up and spend some time digesting. Much Love your way."

"Love will always quiet the sticky situations. Imagine if you will, people consciously wearing a Love mantle. With a good intent, Love will be there in fulfilment

mode activating well being outcomes. Such is the role of Love. When called upon Love does what Love only knows. Remember requests are attended to, when the intent is for well being. It is the only path that functions for Love." "Game time. Relax and enjoy the day."

"Looks like we lost part of our last chat. Not to worry. Gives us a chance to be more specific on what we were about to discuss. Justice. The concept often amuses Me. From My point of view I see it as a launching pad for a pay back time. So many times used to administer punishment. Nothing Loving in that process. Actually like a form of revenge. If the accused had thought carefully of the relevant choices, this situation would not eventuate. Those areas where a capitol punishment is carried out and I am invoked to have mercy on the soul, is literally a joke."

"Back from your little games. Let's get back. Accountability can be such a demand on exclusive rights over individuals. In My domain all I'm interested in is the Evolvement of the individual and to what stage. Punishment is and never been part of My creations. Judgement is like opinions. Nothing tangible only an individual thought about disagreement on choices. Contemplate and digest. Have Love be the sorter out.

Love will and can clarify when called upon when well being is involved."

"A few days since you've answered My calling. So many why's and wherefores going on in your thinking process. Love is about that part of Me available to each and every one of My creations. As I reiterated so many times, Love has no agenda. It oversees and transits when called upon. Anything pertaining to well being. That's why I'm so adamant on calling of Love in each perplexing situation. Love will find the path for any well being situation. Allow It to manifest It's superb attributes. Can see you're getting restless again. Go play at your computer. Much much Love your way."

"All is well in your world? You appear to be more at ease with what we've been chatting about. Keep in mind that with free will, there is responsibility for choices. There is always the opportunity to re choose a choices. Those who seek power for the sake of being in absolute control will use deceitful devices at every opportunity. Constant streaming of falseinformation is the powerful tool used. For the uneducated, choices can be at a minimum. Whatever appeals to a predominant feeling is what can turn people into a flock of sheep, so to *speak. Obedience in this instance is the imperative factor for the one in power to achieve the desired outcome."*

"Forgotten why the contact have you. I AM with you all the time and if you want to chat, I'm here to address the issues. Mon beloved our closeness is dependent on your open channels with Me. I'll await your next chat."

"Thanks for answering the call. I do not go into predictions. I observe Evolvement. Come back tomorrow morning. Much Love.

Freedom. Being in a free mode is absolutely the inner belief. Let's continue tomorrow. When thought is free to roam creativity occurs. Being free to enact the creation is a Love intent of the highest. If tyranny subjects the populace with the intention of control, no matter what, Love will eventually clear a path to enhance a different road. I can see there is anxiety to transfer these chats to the manuscript writings. Lovely to have you in the communication mode. Much Love to you."

"I'm getting anxious on when to put our chatting into book form?" *"All in good time. Allow for the appropriate time to occur. There is no set time in My realm for happenings to happen. Let's wait and see. Once* in motion actuality manifests. Enjoy your day and stay wrapped in your Love mantle."

"Another thing. During this pandemic period, the very thought of Me having anything to do with it, is an insult to My Person. Choices and free will are the main culprits in this episode. How man deals with personal hygiene matters, is their responsibility. Over time education has enlighten a cleaner way in living."

"Dictatorship is another form of subjection. Whether it be from leaders who bully, or in the home life. When one is bullied by another, and coached into the doing of actions against their better self, outcomes can reverberate into much discontent and ill will. Especially when filled with falsehoods and lies to subjugate another. Lack of Love in any action has dire consequences."

"Know that Love is the elements of total connections. Love brings past and future into the NOW. When dealing with fear and doubt, choose Love to bring it all into the present. With Love, openings occur that bring the moment into alignment. Love does what Love does. In perfect harmony. Having had a big break from chatting, has you in a slower receptive mode. Go rest and we'll catch up soon. Much Love your way."

"Good morning I thought we'd start with some recaps. The pandemic going haywire is a cover for what is really going on for a lot of individuals. Another long break. I have the knowing that you would like to come to a conclusion with our chats for the time being. Any urgency to get our chats out into the public arena, isn't on My part. When others express the choice to eaves drop, our chats will drift into their stream of thought. I can see there is a lot of inner editing going on for you. Best to be aware of your choices, go back to when some were made, come into the present and fill those choices with Love. An important process to do. Meanwhile enjoy who you are, clothe yourself constantly with the Love mantle and flow the Love, within, around, through and from you. Much Love to you."

"Don't miss Me too much. I'm always around for you any time."

"Greetings. A long time no write. Do you want to conclude this series? We've been chatting for quite a while. It's been a delight you allowing My Ideas and thoughts to e transposed into the written word. Leave space For future updates. It has been fun, even though you have put yourself Through the mill something. The important message is relationships with LOVE and It's available at all times. When doubts and fears are laid at

Love's door, clarity takes place. Love does not conquer. LOVE assimilates and quietly delights in an outcome. Allow LOVE to be Itself."

"Thank you. It has been quite a journey into a lot of new concepts. I'm glad to have allowed You to have taken up the conversation each morning. It's been fun. Thank you my Godship. Perhaps more at a later date."

"The pleasure is Mine. Enjoy your blessings and enjoy the reactions to these writings. Much LOVE to you."

I felt it was time to conclude this series of chats. It has been one one amazing journey.

I'm still in the land of, what's so or what's not so. I trust the main message of LOVE and all IT'S component parts is of benefit to the reader.

Lastly my gratitude to my darling wife for her wonderful support to have this all happen and actuate. Also to my mentors, Ashtara, Omni and Mahni Dugan, who are wonderful models of much of the LOVE processes. And of course to my GODSHIP, for HIS persistence in being heard.

No doubt there will be more chatting to come. Much LOVE to each and all.

ABOUT THE WRITINGS

Me and My Godship Ava Chat, is a series of inner chats with the writer's personal God. The main theme is one of Love and the ease of having Love embrace the everyday happenings. Free will and choices, plus the responsibilities involved. It is a joyful journey of inner contentment, done with ease.

The intention is to flood the reader with a Love mantle whenever invoked. There is no chronological order, and an intention is that whatever page is opened, a resolution is applicable. It was fun transcribing and perhaps there may be more chats along the way. Enjoy.

Edward J B.

Printed in the United States
By Bookmasters